Camper's Guide to ™
COLORADO

Parks, Lakes, and Forests
Where to Go and How to Get There

Triple waterfall at Rifle Falls State Park

Mickey Little

Gulf Publishing Company

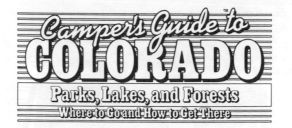

Library of Congress Cataloging-in-Publication Data

Little, Mildred J.
    Camper's guide to Colorado parks, lakes and forests:
—where to go and how to get there/Mickey Little.
      p. cm.
    Includes index.
    ISBN 0-87201-124-0
    1. Camp sites, facilities, etc.—Colorado—Guide-books.
2. Colorado—Description and travel—1981—Guide-books.
I. Title.
GV191.42.C6L58 1990
647.94788—dc20   90-39113
                                         CIP

Also of Interest to Campers—

Camper's Guide to Texas Parks, Lakes, and Forests/Third Edition
Camper's Guide to Florida Parks, Trails, Rivers, and Beaches
Camper's Guide to California Parks, Lakes, Forests, and Beaches
Volume 1: Northern California
Volume 2: Southern California
Camper's Guide to Minnesota Parks, Lakes, Forests, and Trails
Camper's Guide to Outdoor Cooking

Contents

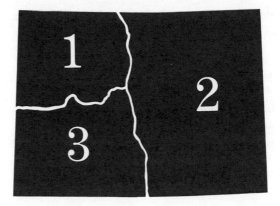

ACKNOWLEDGMENTS ———————————————

I am indebted to and wish to thank the following agencies and individuals for information—in the form of maps, brochures, photographs, telephone conversations, and personal interviews—without which this book would not have been possible.

Colorado Department of Highways
Colorado Division of Parks and Outdoor Recreation
Colorado Division of Wildlife
Colorado Mountain Club
Colorado River Outfitters Association
Colorado Ski Country USA
Colorado Tourism Board
Colorado Trail Foundation
Continental Divide Trail Society
  each District Ranger's office
  each Forest Supervisor's office
Jim and Hazel Gebert
Buddy and Tresa Gilchrest
Mistex Reservation System
National Park Service
Ticketron Reservation System
U.S. Army Corps of Engineers, Albuquerque District
U.S. Army Corps of Engineers, Omaha District
U.S. Bureau of Land Management, Colorado State Office
U.S. Department of the Interior
U.S. Forest Service, Rocky Mountain Region
U.S. Geological Survey

While every effort has been made to ensure the accuracy of the information in this guide, neither I nor the publisher assume liability arising from the use of this material. Park facilities and policies are subject to change, so verify the accuracy of important details before beginning a trip.

Mickey Little

I went to the woods because I wished to live deliberately, to front only the essential facts of life, and see if I could not learn what it had to teach, and not, when I came to die, discover that I had not lived.
—Henry David Thoreau

Introduction

The word "colorado" came from the Spanish "rio colorado," meaning "reddish river." The United States got the eastern and central areas of Colorado as part of the Louisiana Purchase and the western part as a result of the Mexican War. In 1861, the Colorado Territory was established and was a step toward statehood. Colorado entered the Union on August 1, 1876, just as the nation was turning 100 years old, and is thus called the Centennial State. Denver, the capital city, is known as the "Mile-High City," because its elevation is 5,280 feet, that is, one mile above sea level.

Colorado is truly a camper's paradise. The high, dry, sunny climate of Colorado is one of the state's outstanding assets. The state boasts of 300 or more days of sunshine per year. The summer season generally extends from the end of June until early October; about the end of September, the golden yellow high aspen groves are visible for miles. The first snow may fall in September, but at lower elevations it quickly disappears when temperatures

> **Colorado Facts**
> Capital: Denver
> Nicknames: Centennial State; Silver State
> Statehood: August 1, 1876 (38th state)
> Area: 104,247 square miles; ranks 8th
> Population: 3,231,000; ranks 28th
> State Motto: *Nil Sine Numine* (Nothing Without Providence)
> State Bird: Lark Bunting
> State Flower: Rocky Mountain Columbine
> State Tree: Colorado Blue Spruce
> State Animal: Rocky Mountain bighorn sheep
> State Gemstone: Aquamarine
> State Fossil: Stegosaurus
> Local Time: Mountain Time

Happy trails!

approach 70°F. Warm "Indian Summers" often last until December. It's true that from November to early April there is some of the best skiing in the country at more than 30 ski areas, but did you know that folks actually enjoy camping in Colorado 365 days of the year? That's right! In some parks, the activity may change from swimming and sailboarding to ice fishing and cross-country skiing, but the action is still there. Eighteen of the 27 state parks that have camping facilities offer winter camping; many national parks and national forest campgrounds remain open with limited services. So, don't put this *Camper's Guide* in mothballs during the winter; it should prove invaluable year-round!

This *Camper's Guide* suggests places to go and provides directions to get there. You will discover information about the popular, well-known campgrounds as well as the lesser-used camping areas. The public campgrounds presented in this guide, provided and operated by state and federal agencies, afford varied options for outdoor recreation: fishing, boating, canoeing, rafting, backpacking, swimming, sailing, picnicking, bicycling, horseback riding, water skiing, walking along a nature trail, or climbing a "fourteener" (one of Colorado's 54 mountain peaks that are higher than 14,000 ft). In season, you can also downhill ski, cross-country ski, snow shoe, ice skate, ice fish, or snowmobile. You can pursue your favorite hobby as a bird watcher, photographer, botanist, geologist, or naturalist, and your accommodations can range from roughing it in a designated wilderness area to enjoying all the comforts of home in a recreational vehicle. You can spend a day, a weekend, or an entire vacation doing what you like best, no matter how active, or inactive.

The state and federal agency campgrounds in Colorado offer more than 10,000 individual campsites. More than 2,700 campsites are found within the 27 state parks, and the 40 ranger districts within the 11 national forests attribute another 7,600 developed campsites. That doesn't count the campgrounds found at the nine national parks, the several U.S. Army Corps of Engineer lakes, or the BLM (Bureau of Land Management) public lands, where dispersed camping is allowed. No wonder visitors flock to Colorado to fish more than 65,000 miles of streams and more than 2,000 lakes and reservoirs; the season runs almost the year-round and camping spots are plentiful.

Mountains are numerous in Colorado. In fact, there are more than 1,000 peaks that soar at least 10,000 feet.

When you think of Colorado, the first thing that probably comes to mind is mountains! Colorado has six times the mountainous area of Switzerland and has the highest overall elevation of the 50 states, with an average elevation of 6,800 feet. The Rocky Mountains run north-south through the west-central portion of the state. Mount Elbert, about 100 miles southwest of Denver, is the highest point in Colorado with an elevation of 14,433 feet; it is the second highest peak in the contiguous United States. Colorado claims 54 peaks of the 68 peaks over 14,000 feet in the contiguous United States. The lowest point in Colorado is 3,350 feet at the Arkansas River on the Kansas border. The extreme length of Colorado is 387 miles; the extreme breadth is 276 miles.

The Continental Divide splits the state into geographically distinct regions; separating eastern-flowing rivers from those flowing west. The land to the east of this line is sometimes called the Eastern Slope; to the west is called the Western Slope.

Visitors from other states who drive to Colorado should be aware that there are four Colorado Welcome Centers located on major highways entering the state. Not only do the Welcome Centers provide a good rest stop but they also give up-to-date information, brochures, guides, and maps to visitors. The centers are located at the following sites:

—at Burlington, as you travel west from Kansas:
   48265 I-70
   Burlington, CO 80807
   (719) 346-5554
—at Cortez, as you travel north from western New Mexico:
   808 East Main Street (on Highway 160)
   Cortez, CO 81321
   (303) 565-4048
—at Fruita, as you travel east from central Utah:
   340 Highway 340 (Fruita exit on I-70)
   Fruita, CO 81521
   (303) 855-9335
—at Trinidad, as you travel north from central New Mexico:
   309 North Nevada Avenue (Exit 14A on I-25)
   Trinidad, CO 81082
   (719) 846-9512

Prior to a trip, a map and other information such as *Colorado's Official State Vacation Guide* may be obtained from the Colorado Tourism Board. Their address is:

Colorado Tourism Board
1625 Broadway, Suite 1700
Denver CO 80202
(800) 433-2656 (vacation kit)
(303) 592-5410 (business office)

There are rules and regulations encountered at all public campgrounds, whether administered by a state or national agency. Please remember that policies, fees, regulations, and available facilities change from time to time. It's easy for campers to stay informed; merely, request updated information, and when you are camping, read the materials posted or distributed at the park. And, speaking of becoming informed . . . don't quit reading now! The remaining pages of this introduction are packed full of information that will enable you to have and enjoy great camping trips in Colorado for the rest of your life.

HOW TO USE THE CAMPER'S GUIDE

The state is divided into three geographic regions, and the parks, lakes, and forests within each region are arranged alphabetically and are cross-listed by name and city in the index. The first page of each region locates the park, lake, or forest on the map and gives the page number(s) where you can find more detailed information and maps of that specific area.

All the information in this *Camper's Guide* has been supplied by the respective operating agency, either through literature distributed by them, through verbal communication, or through secondary sources deemed reliable. The information presented is basic—it tells you how to get there, cites outstanding features of the area, and lists the facilities and the recreational activities available. Mailing addresses and telephone numbers are given in case you want additional information prior to your trip. For some parks, it's a good idea to confirm weather and road conditions before heading out. Also keep in mind, that during the off-season, some camping areas may be closed or some facilities may be discontinued.

Maps. The maps showing the location of facilities within a park or campground should be of considerable help. These maps are usually available to you at the park headquarters, but they can also aid you in planning a trip to an unfamiliar park. Arriving at a park after dark can be tough if you don't know the

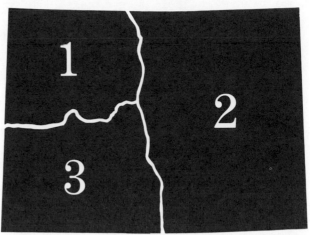

lay-out of the campground. And, those of you who have attempted to meet up with friends at a predetermined spot at a large campground can readily appreciate the value of having such a map. Most parks are easily found with the help of a good road map, but vicinity maps have been included in some instances. Signs along the way can also be relied upon after you reach the general vicinity of a park.

Ranger Districts. Because each ranger district within a national forest operates somewhat independently of the national forest as a whole, distributes its own materials, and in many ways has its own "personality" because of terrain, recreational opportunities, etc., information on each national forest is arranged by ranger districts. Visitors who wish to camp off the beaten path should certainly purchase the official national forest map because even the best road map often does not show the many back roads in the forest. Even with a forest map, there can be confusion when roads change from a county road designation to a forest road designation.

The facilities at a campground are always changing, but a change in status usually means the addition of a service rather than a discontinuation. In other words, a camper often finds better and more facilities than those listed in the latest brochure. During the summer camping season, many parks offer interpretive programs, including nature walks, guided tours, and campfire talks, conducted by park personnel.

May this *Camper's Guide* serve you well in the years ahead, whether you are a beginner or a seasoned camper. Take time to camp, to fish, to hike, and backpack the trails, to become truly acquainted with nature . . . and with yourself, your family, and your friends! Don't put off until tomorrow what can be enjoyed today!

State and federal agencies in Colorado offer more than 10,000 individual campsites at developed campgrounds.

RESERVATION SYSTEMS

Campground reservations are necessary for popular parks in season, i.e., late spring, summer, and early fall. During the non-reservation periods family campsites are available on a first-come, first-served basis; this is the same basis for unreserved campsites during the reservation period. The list of parks/campgrounds requiring reservations and their reservation season may change from year to year. Even the agency handling the reservations can change. Perhaps, the best procedure for a campground user is, each year, to obtain up-to-date brochures describing the reservation procedure and containing the camping reservation application. The brochure also serves as a valuable source of information on fees and facilities available. Remember that the reservation system differs for state parks, national parks, and national forests.

State Parks

At present, all 27 state parks are on the Mistix reservation system. The peak season for most parks is Memorial Day through Labor Day; reservations are advised for the most popular parks. Reservations for group campgrounds and the cabins at Colorado State Forest can also be made through Mistix. Weather permitting, most parks keep some sites open throughout the year. Contact the park office or Mistix for campsite availability information. You may make a reservation up to 120 days in advance or as late as 2 to 7 days prior to your arrival. Up to three sites may be reserved for any one date of arrival. Visa and Mastercard are accepted with phone reservations: Visa, Mastercard, personal checks, and money orders are accepted with mail-in reservations. There is a reservation charge. Calls are taken 8 to 5 on weekdays and 9 to noon on weekends.

For the *Information and Reservation Application* and for camping reservations, contact:

Mistix
P.O. Box 315
10065 East Harvard
Denver, CO 80231
(303) 671-4500 (Denver)
1-800-365-CAMP

National Parks

Only one national park in Colorado is on the reservation system through Ticketron. Rocky Mountain National Park has two of its five campgrounds on this system: Moraine Park and Glacier Basin. These two popular parks have a 7-night limit between June 1 and September 30. The other three campgrounds are on a first-come, first-served basis.

Phone reservations, call:
(213) 410-1720
(303) 825-8447 or
(602) 340-9033

For the Ticketron *Family Campsite Reservations* brochure, contact:

Ticketron
Dept. R
401 Hackensack Ave.
Hackensack, NJ 07601

National Forests

Selected national forests throughout the United States have recently adopted a reservation system through a San Diego-based Mistix corporation. A list of the national forest campgrounds on the reservation system can be obtained from the forest supervisor at any of the 11 national forests in Colorado. Due to popularity of campgrounds, this list could possibly change from year to year. Reservations are advised for these selected campgrounds during peak seasons; for most campgrounds, this is Memorial Day through Labor Day. Other campgrounds will still operate entirely on a first-come, first-served basis. Weather permitting, most ranger districts keep some sites open after Labor Day. For campsite availability information, call the appropriate ranger district office. You may make reservations up to 120 days in advance of your first night of arrival, for family sites and 360 days for group sites, or as late at 10 days prior to your arrival (3 days for some group campgrounds). Visa and Mastercard are accepted with phone reservations; Visa, Mastercard, personal checks and money orders are accepted with mail-in reservations. There is a reservation charge. Calls are taken 9 to 6 on weekdays, and 9 to 2 on weekends, Pacific Standard Time.

For the *Information and Reservation Application* and for camping reservations, contact:

Mistix
P.O. Box 85705
San Diego, CA 92138-5705
1-800-283-CAMP

STATE PARKS

Colorado's state parks are located in all types of settings: the flat eastern slope of the Great Plains, and the mountainous western slope with its high peaks and deep gorges; along rivers and on lakes; along the busy Interstate Highway-25 near "civilization," and along a dirt road, off-the-beaten-path, and miles from anywhere. Each park offers its own unique opportunities for fun and adventure. Colorado has 35 state parks, all administered by the Colorado Division of Parks and Outdoor Recreation. Actually, only 12 of them are called "state parks," 22 are called "state recreation areas," and one is a "state forest." Henceforth, they all will be referred to simply as "state parks." Eight of the parks are for day-use only, but the other 27 state parks have camping facilities and receive major emphasis in this *Camper's Guide.*

Camping accommodations differ greatly. Eleven Mile has 274 campsites and Pueblo has 214, while Rifle Falls just has 18 and Paonia has 16. At the latest count, the number of campsites available at Colorado state parks totals 2,741. Of the 25 parks with campsites, 12 provide showers, 7 have electricity hook-ups available, 22 have dump stations, and 9 have group campgrounds available. Eighteen of the parks indicate that they provide opportunities for winter camping. The parks located on the eastern slope near I-25 tend to provide the most extensive facilities. This is probably understandable because an estimated two-thirds of the state's population live in this area.

Backpacking in Colorado's 670-mile section of the Continental Divide trail requires planning, good equipment, and stamina (see page 15)—but the rewards are priceless.

The parks vary in size from 40-acre Rifle Falls and 50-acre Barbour Ponds to 17,035-acre Pueblo and 70,708-acre State Forest. Island Acres boasts just 10 acres of water, while Navajo has access to 15,600 acres of water. Elevations range from 3,700 feet at Bonny Reservoir near the Kansas border to 10,000 feet at State Forest. Actually, 26 of the 35 Colorado state parks are located at altitudes more than a mile high.

The 35 Colorado state parks provide the setting for a wide variety of recreational activities. Consider the following facts:

—16 parks have swimming facilities
—33 parks have fishing opportunities, either stream, river, or lake
—10 parks have marinas
—26 parks have areas suitable for sailboarding
—19 parks have areas suitable for water skiing
—28 parks have areas for cross-country skiing
—3 parks have model airplane fields
—5 parks have rock climbing areas
—22 parks allow horseback riding; 12 of them have trails that total over 250 miles
—9 parks have bicycle trails that total nearly 200 miles
—24 parks have hiking trails that total over 275 miles

This *Camper's Guide* contains detailed information on facilities and activities available at each state park. Each year various parks may upgrade and/or add facilities and services. To keep abreast of these changes, obtain the latest copy of *Colorado At Its Best,* the free brochure on the state parks, published by the Colorado Division of Parks and Recreation. You may also want to obtain the individual park brochure on any that you plan to visit. These are available free through individual parks; addresses have been included:

Colorado Division of Parks and Outdoor
  Recreation
1313 Sherman St. #618
Denver, CO 80203
(303) 866-3437

State Park Permits and Fees

A valid park pass is required on every vehicle entering a state park. A daily pass is $3; an annual pass, good for the entire calendar year at all state parks, is $30. Residents of Colorado, who are 62 years of age or older, pay $5 for the annual pass. Camping permits are $6 or $7 per night, depending on the facilities available. Electrical hookups, available at just 7 parks, are $3 per night.

State Park Regulations

State parks are open year-round, weather permitting. Most parks attempt to keep at least some campsites open during the fall and winter months. Day use areas are generally open from 5 a.m. to 10 p.m. and, when they are open, campgrounds are open 24 hours a day. Advance reservations may be made for family campsites, group campgrounds, and primitive cabins in Colorado's state parks. For details on the reservation system, see page 4.

A brochure entitled *Colorado State Park Regulations*, available free from the Colorado Division of Parks and Outdoor Recreation states that "the purpose of these regulations is to provide maximum recreational opportunity on the state's natural, scenic, and recreation areas while also protecting, preserving, and managing these areas for the benefit and enjoyment of the citizens and visitors of this state." The brochure spells out in detail numerous regulations; only a few are cited here. Although some parks have regulations unique to their special situations, the following highlights are basic to most parks:

△ All pets must be kept on a leash no longer than six feet; pets are not permitted on swim beaches or certain other areas.
△ A valid park pass is required on all motorized vehicles.
△ Swimming is permitted only in designated areas.
△ Camping is permitted in designated areas with a valid camping permit. A camping permit is necessary in addition to a park pass.
△ Motorists should obey traffic regulations, and should park only in designated areas and drive only on designated roads.
△ Fires are permitted in grills only. Grills or fire rings are provided in picnic and camping areas.
△ Glass containers are not permitted on swimming beaches.
△ It is unlawful to damage, destroy, remove or litter any property.

NATIONAL PARKS

There are ten national park areas in Colorado: these include one national recreation area, one national historic site, two national parks, and six national monuments. The word "park" is henceforth used as a general term to refer to all of the national areas. Two of the parks, Bent's Old Fort National Historic Site and Florissant Fossil Beds National Monument, do not have camping facilities, so information on them is not included in this book. Two other parks, Hovenweep National Monument and Dinosaur National Monument extend into Utah; because their campgrounds are actually located in Utah, information is excluded. However, you will want to keep these four parks in mind as you travel through Colorado as they are great parks to visit.

Of the six national parks that offer camping in Colorado, one is located in Region 1, one in Region 2, and four in Region 3. Information on camping that is basic to national parks in general is cited here rather than repeated for each park.

△ All parks have a visitor/information center containing interpretive displays and, sometimes, museums pertaining to that park. Most sell literature with in-depth explanations of history, geology, flora, and fauna. Usually an introductory film or slide show is offered.
△ The visitor/information center should always be your first stop; brochures, maps, and a schedule of activities are readily available.
△ Both entrance fees and recreation use fees are authorized at many park areas. Entrance fees are not charged visitors 12 years of age or younger or 62 years of age or older. (See page 8 for "Federal Recreation Passport Program.")

Hovenweep National Monument is located along the Utah-Colorado border, and the campgrounds are actually in Utah. All of the approach roads to these Pre-Columbian Indian ruins are graded dirt roads.

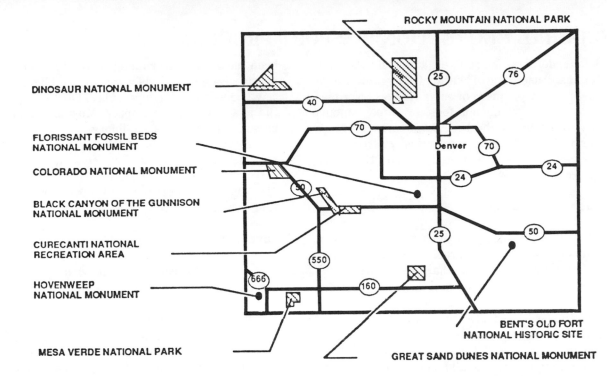

DINOSAUR NATIONAL MONUMENT

FLORISSANT FOSSIL BEDS
NATIONAL MONUMENT

COLORADO NATIONAL MONUMENT

BLACK CANYON OF THE GUNNISON
NATIONAL MONUMENT

CURECANTI NATIONAL
RECREATION AREA

HOVENWEEP
NATIONAL MONUMENT

MESA VERDE NATIONAL PARK

ROCKY MOUNTAIN NATIONAL PARK

Denver

BENT'S OLD FORT
NATIONAL HISTORIC SITE

GREAT SAND DUNES NATIONAL MONUMENT

△ Campsite users are charged recreation use fees at all campgrounds that have certain minimum facilities and services during season. The season varies with the park, but fees are usually collected from April or May through September or October. After the camping season, when water and flush toilets may not be available, no fees are charged. Some campgrounds may be closed during the off-season.

△ Facilities at some national parks may be operated by concessionaires. If they are, the fees they charge are not federal recreation use fees so they are not affected by the Golden Eagle, Golden Access, or Golden Age Passports.

△ Individual campsites are available on a first-come, first-served basis and cannot be reserved. An exception to this is that for the summer camping season, reservations can be made through Ticketron for two of the campgrounds at Rocky Mountain National Park: Moraine Park Campground and Glacier Basin Campground. See page 4, for details on the reservation system.

△ Some parks have campgrounds available for organized groups or other large parties; reservations for these should be made with the individual park.

△ The length of stay in most parks is 14 days; during the off-season it may be longer. An exception to this is a parkwide 7-day limit and a 3-day limit at Longs Peak Campground at Rocky Mountain National Park from June 1 through September 30.

△ Primitive camping is permitted in many of the remote, roadless areas, but occasionally backcountry use is prohibited. Contact the specific park for information about backcountry restrictions. Backcountry permits are free, but are usually required.

△ Many parks have campgrounds that meet the needs of visitors in wheelchairs. Disabled visitors who have questions about their ability to use a particular campground should write to that park for more information.

△ In many parks, interpretive programs, including nature walks, guided tours, and campfire talks are conducted by park personnel.

△ Every area of a park is a museum of natural or human history; removal or destruction of any feature is not allowed. The ideal visitor "takes nothing but memories, leaves nothing but footprints."

△ Hunting is prohibited in national parks; fishing requires a state fishing license.

△ Pets are allowed in the parks and campgrounds if they are kept on a leash or under other physical restraint at all times. They are generally prohibited in backcountry areas.

For further information, contact:

National Park Service
12795 W. Almeda Parkway
Lakewood, CO 80225
(303) 969-2000

FEDERAL RECREATION PASSPORT PROGRAM

Some federal parks, refuges, and facilities can be entered and used free of charge. Other areas and facilities require payment of entrance fees, user fees, special recreation permit fees, or some combination. A brochure by the U.S. Department of the Interior entitled *Federal Recreation Passport Program* explains the five programs. Briefly stated, they are as follows:

Golden Eagle Passport

An annual entrance pass to those national parks, monuments, historic sites, recreation areas, and national wildlife refuges that charge entrance fees. It admits the permit holder and accompanying persons in a private, noncommercial vehicle. For those not traveling by private car, it admits the permit holder and family group. Cost, $25; good for one calendar year (January 1 through December 31); permits unlimited entries to all federal entrance fee areas.

Golden Age Passport

A free lifetime entrance pass for citizens or permanent residents of the United States who are 62 years or older. Also provides 50% discount on federal use fees charged for facilities and services except those provided by private concessionaires. Must to obtained in person, with proof of age.

Golden Access Passport

A free lifetime entrance pass for citizens or permanent residents of the United States who have been medically determined to be blind or permanently disabled and, as a result, are eligible to receive benefits under federal law. Offers same benefits as Golden Age Passport. Must be obtained in person, with proof of eligibility.

Locations where these three passes are obtainable include all National Park System areas where entrance fees are charged, all National Forest Service supervisor's offices, and most Forest Service ranger station offices.

Park Pass

An annual entrance permit to a specific park, monument, historic site, or recreation area in the National Park System that charges entrance fees. The park pass is valid for entrance fees only and does not cover use fees. Cost is $10 or $15, depending upon the area; good for one calendar year (January 1 through December 31); permits unlimited entries only to the park unit where it is purchased.

Federal Duck Stamp

Officially known as the Migratory Bird Hunting and Conservation Stamp and still required of waterfowl hunters, the federal Duck Stamp now also serves as an annual entrance fee permit to national wildlife refuges that charge entrance fees. The Duck Stamp is valid for entrance fees only and does not cover use fees. Cost, $10; good from July 1 through June 30 of the following year; permits unlimited entries to all national wildlife refuges that charge entrance fees. Can be purchased at most post offices.

NATIONAL FORESTS

Colorado's 11 national forests, covering nearly 14 million acres, of the Rocky Mountain Region are managed by the Forest Service of the U.S. Department of Agriculture. The Forest Service is dedicated to multiple-use management for the sustained yield of renewable resources such as water, forage, wildlife, wood, and recreation. This multiple-use management is directed by a forest supervisor. In Colorado, there are seven forest supervisors because several of the forests are administratively combined. The Gunnison, Grand Mesa, and Uncompahgre national forests were administratively combined in 1976. Arapaho and Roosevelt national forests are also combined administratively, as well as

National forest lands, such as Arapaho National Forest pictured here, offer thousands of miles of trails suitable for hiking and backpacking.

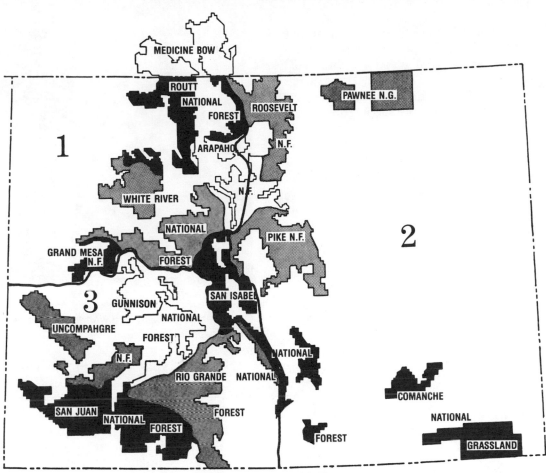

Colorado's National Forests

Pike and San Isabel national forests. Each national forest is divided into districts, averaging about 250,000 acres, with a district ranger responsible for multiple-use administration for the district. The best source of specific and local information is the district ranger's or forest supervisor's office administering the area. For your convenience, addresses and phone numbers for these offices are included in this *Camper's Guide* for each national forest. Location of the regional office is:

U.S. Forest Service
Rocky Mountain Region
11177 W. 8th Ave.
P.O. Box 25127
Lakewood, CO 80225
(303) 236-9431

Because each ranger district within a national forest operates somewhat independently of the national forest as a whole, distributes its own materials, and in many ways has its own "personality" because of terrain, recreational opportunities, etc., information on each national forest in this *Camper's Guide* is arranged by ranger districts. Visitors to a

national forest are encouraged to visit either the office of the forest supervisor or the individual ranger district office. They are able to supply you with numerous brochures on the various recreational activities, as well as give information on such items as road conditions, weather, campgrounds, dispersed camping, and trails. Those who wish to camp off-the-beaten-path should consider purchasing the official national forest map because even the best road map often does not show the many back roads in the forest. Even with a forest map, there can be confusion when roads change from a county road designation to a forest road designation. Forest maps are $2.00 each and may be purchased from either the Forest Service Regional Office, or the appropriate forest supervisor or ranger district.

Information that is basic to all national forests is given here rather than repeated for each forest. For specific information on campground locations and facilities, refer to the appropriate national forest.

△ Forest Service campgrounds are usually open from May 30 through Labor Day weekend. After Labor Day many campgrounds remain open but water systems are turned off and visitors are asked to pack their own trash out (contact district office for closures).

△ A typical campground will have individual parking spaces (most accommodate trailers averaging 18 feet in length), tables and fireplaces, and a central water supply. Most of the campgrounds have vault toilet facilities.

△ Most campsites are available on a first-come, first-served basis. Recently, some 80 forest campgrounds were placed on the reservation system with Mistix. For details of the reservation system, see page 4. The limit of stay varies from 1 to 14 days. Fees range from $4.00 to $10.00 a day and are paid at the campground.

△ Campfires for cooking and warming are generally permitted on national forest land. Fires may be restricted or prohibited in certain areas. Signs will be posted in the areas affected. Within camp and picnic grounds, campfires may be built only in the grates provided.

△ Bring a portable stove to use in case open fires are prohibited or firewood scarce. Only dead wood lying on the ground may be gathered for campfires; do not cut standing timber, bushes, or vegetation.

△ Please, be careful with fire. Campfires must be attended at all times and completely extinguished before leaving.

△ Fishing and hunting in compliance with state laws are allowed on National Forests and Grasslands. Possession of a valid state license is required.

Campfires for cooking and warming are generally permitted on national forest land; use only fallen timber for firewood.

△ Various types of insects are present in the Rocky Mountains. Wood ticks are common during the spring months (April through July). The bite of a wood tick can cause Colorado tick fever or Rocky Mountain spotted fever. A check over the entire body should be made at least once a day.

△ Pets are allowed in national forests. In developed recreation sites, along designated trails and within certain wilderness areas, regulations require that dogs be kept on a leash no longer than six feet in length.

△ Most roads identified as "all weather" on the visitor maps are suitable for passenger cars and vehicles pulling trailers. Roads identified as "dirt" may not be suitable for sedans or vehicles pulling trailers. "Primitive" and "4-wheel" roads may be passable only with 4-wheel drive vehicles. Local inquiry should be made concerning the condition of "dirt," "primitive," or "4-wheel" roads.

△ The only poisonous snake in the Rocky Mountain Region is the rattlesnake. It is generally found at elevations under 7,000 feet.

△ Water from developed systems at recreation sites is safe to drink. Open water sources are easily contaminated by human or animal waste. Water from springs, lakes, ponds, and streams should be treated. A recommended method of treatment is to bring clear water to a rolling boil for five minutes.

△ The elevation of the forests in the Rocky Mountain Region ranges from 5,000 feet to 14,000 feet. Most of the campgrounds are be-

A typical campsite at a national forest developed campground has an individual parking space, a tent pad, table, and fire grill.

tween 5,400 feet and 12,000 feet. Persons coming from lower elevations should be aware that time is needed to adjust to higher elevations. The time necessary to adapt depends on the elevational change and a person's physical condition.

△ Warm days and cool to freezing nights can be expected in the Rocky Mountains during the summer. July and August are usually the warmest months. During this time, afternoon thunderstorms are common. Come prepared for both warm and chilly weather, as well as for rain showers.

△ As a user of national forest system lands, you have significant responsibility for your personal safety during any activity you might pursue. It is your responsibility to know the hazards involved in your activities and to use the proper safety procedures and equipment to minimize the inherent risks and hazards related to your activity.

BACKCOUNTRY ETHICS

Rules imposed by those who administer the various backcountry areas are common sense rules meant to control actions that may damage natural resources. In recent years, the term "going light" has taken on new meaning. To a backpacker, "going light" is the skill of paring down the load and leaving at home every ounce that can be spared. But "going light" also means to spare the land and travel and camp by the rules of "low impact." The National Forest Service suggests the following "low-impact" rules. Although these suggestions were written for the hiker and backpacker, they are quite appropriate for anyone using the backcountry, whether they are traveling by foot, canoe, bicycle, or horse.

General Information

1. Don't short-cut trails. Trails are designed and maintained to prevent erosion.
2. Cutting across switchbanks and trampling meadows can create a confusing maze of unsightly trails.
3. Don't pick flowers, dig up plants, or cut branches from live trees. Leave them for others to see and enjoy.

Plan Your Trip

1. Keep your party small.
2. Take a gas stove to help conserve firewood.
3. Bring sacks to carry out your trash.
4. Take a light shovel or trowel to help with personal sanitation.
5. Carry a light basin or collapsible bucket for washing.
6. Check on weather conditions and water availability.
7. Before your hike, study maps of the area, get permits if necessary, and learn the terrain.

Setting Up Camp

1. Pick a campsite where you won't need to clear away vegetation or level a tent site.

If all trail users refrained from littering, trails would remain as beautiful as this one.

2. Use an existing campsite, if available.
3. Camp 300 feet from streams or springs. Law prohibits camping within ¼ mile of an only available water source (for wildlife or livestock).
4. Do not cut trees, limbs or brush to make camp improvements. Carry own tent poles.

Breaking Camp

1. Before leaving camp, naturalize the area. Replace rocks and wood used; scatter needles, leaves, and twigs on the campsite.
2. Scout the area to be sure you've left nothing behind. Everything you packed into your camp should be packed out. Try to make it appear as if no one had been there.

Campfires

1. Use gas stoves when possible to conserve dwindling supplies of firewood.
2. If you need to build a fire, use an existing campfire site. Keep it small. Before you leave, make sure it is out.

Those camping by the rules of "low impact" pick a campsite where they don't need to rearrange the natural area.

3. If you need to clear a new fire site, select a safe spot away from rock ledges that would be blackened by smoke; away from meadows where it would destroy grass and leave a scar; away from dense brush, trees and duff, where it would be a fire hazard.
4. Clear a circle of all burnable materials. Dig a shallow pit for the fires. Keep the sod intact.
5. Use only fallen timber for firewood. Even standing dead trees are part of the beauty of wilderness, and are important to wildlife.
6. Put your fire cold out before leaving, let the fire burn down to ashes, mix the ashes with dirt and water. Feel it with your hand. If it's cold out, cover the ashes in the pit with dirt, replace the sod, and naturalize the disturbed area. Rockfire rings, if needed or used, should be scattered before leaving.

Pack It In—Pack It Out

1. Bring trash bags to carry out all trash that cannot be completely burned.
2. Aluminum foil and aluminum lined packages won't burn up in your fire. Compact it and put it in your trash bag.

3. Cigarette butts, pull-tags, and gum wrappers are litter, too. They can spoil a campsite and trail.
4. Don't bury trash! Animals dig it up.
5. Try to pack out trash left by others. Your good example may catch on!

Keep The Water Supply Clean

1. Wash yourself, your dishes, and your clothes in a container.
2. Pour wash water on the ground away from streams and springs.
3. Food scraps, tooth paste, even biodegradable soap will pollute streams and springs. Remember, it's your drinking water, too!
4. Boil water or treat water before drinking it.

Disposing of Human Waste

1. When nature calls, select a suitable spot at least 100 feet from open water, campsites, and trails. Dig a hole 4 to 6 inches deep. Try to keep the sod intact.
2. After use, fill in the hole, completely burying waste. Then tramp in the sod.

Emergency Items

1. According to conditions, carry extra warm clothing such as windbreakers, wool jackets, hats, and gloves. Keep extra high-energy foods like hard candies, chocolate, dried fruits, or liquids accessible. Don't overload yourself, but be prepared for emergencies.
2. Travel with a first aid kit, map, compass, and whistle. Know how to use them.
3. Always leave your trip plan with a member of your family or a close friend.
4. Mishaps are rare, but they do happen. Should one occur, remain calm. In case of an accident, someone should stay with the injured person. Notify the nearest state, local, or federal law enforcement office for aid.

WILDERNESS AREAS

There is no wonder that wilderness areas in Colorado's national forests attract more and more visitors each year as they offer something for everyone: rugged mountain slopes for experienced mountaineers; placid lakes for family campers; and a solitary get-away for people seeking isolation. Although many nonwilderness areas in the national forests provide similar opportunities for camping and hiking in an isolated, undeveloped setting, wilderness areas in particular are managed to preserve their natural conditions. In years past we spoke of the ability of man to survive the wilderness; now, we speak of wilderness as the land's capability of surviving man. The best way to help the land survive is to make the least possible impact on the environment. Visitors are asked to observe notrace camping practices in order to leave areas as undisturbed as possible.

Twenty-five wilderness areas are in 10 of the 11 national forests in Colorado. Grand Mesa National Forest is the only national forest that lacks a designated wilderness area, while 7 are in the White River National Forest. Gunnison and Roosevelt each have 5, Arapaho and Routt have 4; Rio

Grande, San Isabel, San Juan and Uncompahgre each have 3; and Pike National Forest has 2. Three national parks have wilderness areas: namely, Black Canyon of the Gunnison, Great Sand Dunes and Mesa Verde.

Be sure to obtain a map of the national forest you intend to visit; they are available for $2.00 each from the appropriate Forest Supervisor's Office or from:

U.S. Forest Service
Rocky Mountain Region
11177 West 8th Avenue
P.O. Box 25127
Lakewood, CO 80225
(303) 236-9431

USGS topographic quad maps are available for many of the wilderness areas, either from Colorado camping suppliers or from the U.S. Geological Survey office in Denver. A free index map to select the quad map(s) you may need for your trip is also available from USGS:

U.S. Geological Survey
Denver Federal Center
P.O. Box 25046
Mail Stop 504
Denver, CO 80225
(303) 236-5829

A visitor permit is no longer required to enter the wilderness areas. However, you should check with the appropriate national forest to determine access points and to obtain the latest information on travel conditions and wilderness regulations for that particular wilderness area. Although some regulations are basic to all wilderness areas, some may vary from area to area. An alphabetical list of the 25 wilderness areas in Colorado, along with the names of the national forests in which they are located, is presented here for general information. Refer to the appropriate national forest in the main body of this book for a short description of each of the wilderness areas, regarding size and type of terrain.

Wilderness Areas by National Forests

Big Blue Wilderness—Uncompahgre, p. 151
Cache La Poudre Wilderness—Roosevelt, p. 97
Collegiate Peaks Wilderness—Gunnison, p. 124; San Isabel, pp. 112, 141; White River, p. 56
Comanche Peak Wilderness—Roosevelt, p. 98
Eagles Nest Wilderness—Arapaho, p. 24; White River, p. 56
Flat Tops Wilderness—Routt, p. 38; White River, p. 56

This youngster is enjoying winter camping in the Maroon Bells-Snowmass Wilderness Area. See page 17 for more snow activities.

Holy Cross Wilderness—San Isabel, pp. 112, 141; White River, p. 56
Hunter-Fryingpan Wilderness—White River, p. 56
Indian Peaks Wilderness—Arapaho, p. 24; Roosevelt, p. 98
LaGarita Wilderness—Gunnison, p. 124; Rio Grande, p. 135
Lizard Head Wilderness—San Juan, p. 145; Uncompahgre, p. 151
Lost Creek Wilderness—Pike, p. 85
Maroon Bells-Snowmass Wilderness—Gunnison, p. 124; White River, p. 56
Mt. Evans Wilderness—Arapaho, p. 24; Pike, p. 85
Mt. Massive Wilderness—San Isabel, pp. 112, 141
Mt. Sneffels Wilderness—Uncompahgre, p. 151
Mt. Zirkel Wilderness—Routt, p. 38
Neota Wilderness—Roosevelt, p. 98
Never Summer Wilderness—Arapaho, p. 24; Routt, p. 38
Platte River Wilderness—Routt, p. 38
Raggeds Wilderness—Gunnison, p. 124; White River, p. 56
Rawah Wilderness—Roosevelt, p. 98
South San Juan Wilderness—Rio Grande, p. 135; San Juan, p. 145
Weminuche Wilderness—Rio Grande, p. 135; San Juan, p. 145
West Elk Wilderness—Gunnison, p. 124

COLORADO MOUNTAIN PEAKS

According to the state's *Official State Vacation Guide*, Colorado has the highest overall elevation of the 50 states, with an average altitude of 6,800 feet and has six times the mountainous area of Switzerland. The state contains 75% of all the area in the continental United States with an elevation of more than 10,000 feet above sea level. In fact, there are more than 1,000 peaks that soar at least 10,000 feet.

In the contiguous United States, there are 68 peaks that surpass 14,000 feet; 54 of them are located in Colorado. Hikers and climbers consider these "fourteeners" a special challenge; many spend their weekends and vacations trying to "bag" them all. The highest point in Colorado is 14,433-foot Mount Elbert, southwest of Leadville. Sunshine Peak, at an elevation of 14,001 feet, is the lowest of the "fourteeners." The official state map, prepared by the Colorado Department of Highways, displays a list of the 54 peaks according to height; map locations are also given. Because 46 of the "fourteeners" are located on national forest lands and camping in the national forests is a major part of this camper's guide, the "fourteeners" are listed here according to the national forest in which they are located. Note that in some instances the mountain peak is listed for two national forests, indicating that the peak is located on the boundary. Listing the peaks in this manner should aid the hiker/climber in obtaining information pertinent to the climb.

At 14,150-feet, Mt. Sneffels, in the Uncompahgre National Forest, is one of Colorado's 54 "fourteeners."

Colorado's Fourteeners

Name of Peak	Altitude	National Forest(s)
Grays Peak	14,270	Arapaho
Torreys Peak	14,267	Arapaho
Quandary Peak	14,265	Arapaho
Mt. Evans	14,264	Arapaho & Pike
Castle Peak	14,265	Gunnison & White River
San Luis Peak	14,014	Gunnison
Mt. Lincoln	14,286	Pike
Mt. Bross	14,172	Pike
Mt. Democrat	14,148	Pike & San Isabel
Pikes Peak	14,110	Pike
Mt. Bierstadt	14,060	Pike
Blanca Peak	14,345	Rio Grande & San Isabel
Crestone Peak	14,294	Rio Grande
Crestone Needle	14,191	Rio Grande & San Isabel
Ellingwood Peak	14,042	Rio Grande & San Isabel

Name of Peak	Altitude	National Forest(s)
Little Bear Peak	14,037	Rio Grande
Mt. Elbert	14,433	San Isabel
Mt. Massive	14,421	San Isabel
Mt. Harvard	14,420	San Isabel
LaPlata Peak	14,336	San Isabel
Mt. Antero	14,269	San Isabel
Mt. Shavano	14,229	San Isabel
Mt. Belford	14,197	San Isabel
Mt. Princeton	14,197	San Isabel
Mt. Yale	14,196	San Isabel
Tabeguache Mtn.	14,155	San Isabel
Mt. Oxford	14,153	San Isabel
Mt. Columbia	14,073	San Isabel
Missouri Mountain	14,067	San Isabel
Humboldt Peak	14,064	San Isabel
Huron Peak	14,005	San Isabel
Mt. Wilson	14,246	San Juan
El Diente Peak	14,159	San Juan
Mt. Eolus	14,083	San Juan
Windom Peak	14,082	San Juan
Sunlight Peak	14,059	San Juan
Uncompahgre Peak	14,309	Uncompahgre
Mt. Sneffels	14,150	Uncompahgre
Wetterhorn Peak	14,017	Uncompahgre
Wilson Peak	14,017	Uncompahgre
South Maroon Peak	14,156	White River
Capitol Peak	14,130	White River
Snowmass Mountain	14,092	White River
Pyramid Peak	14,018	White River
North Maroon Peak	14,014	White River
Mt. of the Holy Cross	14,005	White River

Just eight of Colorado's 54 "fourteeners" are located on lands other than the national forests. General locations are listed below:

Longs Peak   14,256   Rocky Mountain N.P.

Kit Carson Peak   14,165   below & west of San Isabel N.F. & near Rio Grande N.F.)

Culebra Peak   14,069   near New Mexico border

Handies Peak   14,048   north of Rio Grande N.F.

Mt. Lindsey   14,042   south of San Isabel N.F.

Mt. Sherman   14,036   near Pike N.F. & San Isabel N.F.

Redcloud Peak   14,034   north of San Juan N.F.

Sunshine Peak   14,001   north of San Juan N.F.

The location of each peak was determined directly from U.S.G.S. topographical maps. The altitude listed for each of the mountain peaks is according to data from the Colorado Mountain Club. This organization is an excellent source of information on the "fourteeners."

Colorado Mountain Club
2530 West Alameda
Denver, CO 80219
(303) 922-8315

CONTINENTAL DIVIDE TRAIL

The Continental Divide National Scenic Trail, formally established by the National Parks and Recreation Act of November 10, 1978, is similar in concept to the Pacific Crest Trail and the Appalachian Trail. When completed, the Continental Divide Trail will follow the Rocky Mountains and extend 3,000 miles from the Canadian border in Montana to the border of Mexico in New Mexico. About 1,900 miles of corridor contains existing trails or primitive routes. The corridor varies from 4,000 feet to over 13,000 feet above mean sea level. The proposed route traverses a variety of terrain, including high desert, forest land, alpine, interesting geological formations, and high mountain meadows. It also crosses a variety of land ownerships.

Much of Colorado's 670 miles of the trail is already in place on national forest lands. This is high country, often in wilderness areas, and requires planning, good equipment, and stamina. The route can be followed, though, with the help of good maps. One source of information is the series *Guide to the Continental Divide Trail*. Two books, one on northern Colorado and one on southern Colorado, are published by and available from:

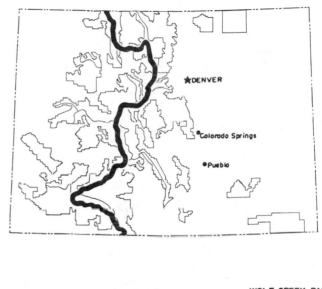

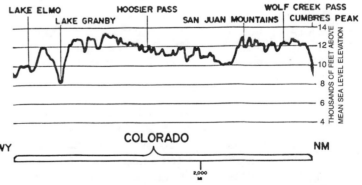

Continental Divide Trail Society
P.O. Box 30002
Bethesda, Maryland 20814

Another guidebook is *Colorado's Continental Divide* by Ron Ruhoff, published by Cordillera Press, Inc., Box 3699, Evergreen, CO 80439.

Locally, information can be obtained from:

Colorado Mountain Club
2530 W. Alameda
Denver, CO 80219
(303) 922-8315

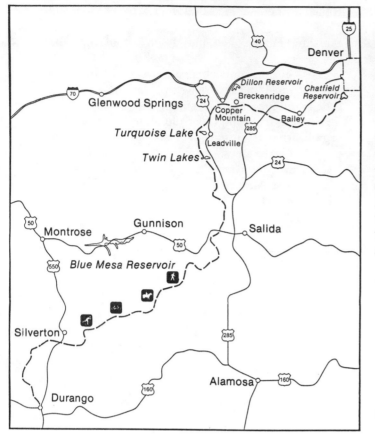

The Colorado Trail is a 470-mile recreational trail that crosses Colorado from Denver to Durango, traversing seven national forests, six wilderness areas, five major river systems, and eight mountain ranges. The trail crosses the Continental Divide several times and provides the traveler some of the most spectacular scenery in the Rocky Mountains. Begun in 1973, and sponsored by the Friends of the Colorado Trail, the Colorado Mountain Club, and the U.S. Forest Service, most work has been by volunteers. Volunteer efforts are still needed for trail construction projects; contact the Colorado Trail Foundation. *A Colorado High*, the official guide to the Colorado Trail, as well as a complete set of 29 topographic maps for the Colorado Trail, are available from:

The Colorado Trail Foundation
P.O. Box 260876
Lakewood, CO 80226-0876
(303) 526-0809

BLM PUBLIC LANDS

Public lands administered by the Bureau of Land Management (BLM), an agency in the U.S. Department of the Interior, offer countless recreational opportunities for millions of people every year. The BLM public lands are those lands obtained by the federal government over the past 200 years through purchase or treaty that have remained in federal ownership, but are not part of an established national park or forest, wildlife refuge, or military reservation. More than eight million acres of public lands in Colorado are managed by the BLM. Nearly all of these lands lie at intermediate elevations between privately-owned mountain valleys and the higher forested areas.

BLM's basic mission is to manage the public lands for maximum public good both now and in the future, following principles of multiple use management. Until passage of the Federal Land Policy and Management Act in 1976, BLM had no clear directive to provide for outdoor recreation use. This clear mandate given to BLM brought another dimension to public land management. It recognized

recreation as a major resource management program. BLM in Colorado is now developing the capability to deliver specific kinds of recreation opportunities and to provide visitor services to public users.

Once thought of as the "Lands Nobody Wanted," leftover from the original public domain, the public lands have become the place to go for unconfined recreation. Colorado's public lands offer residents and visitors alike a wide variety of recreation. These range from back country hiking or wilderness rafting to picnicking or trailbiking in more developed areas. In BLM's free booklet, *Colorado Recreation Opportunity Guide*, the location and facilities at 20 developed recreation sites are presented. Of the 15 recreation sites that allow camping, all of them are rather small; three are listed as primitive sites; and only three have drinking water. The peak use season usually runs from about Memorial Day through Labor Day weekend and also includes big game hunting seasons. Though most of the developed sites are open all year, some at higher elevations are closed during the off-season. BLM's developed recreation sites vary in their accommodations and are filled on a first-come, first-served basis. Reservations are not taken. Fees are being charged for camping in some but not all BLM's developed sites. Except where specifically prohibited, camping is allowed outside the developed sites; fees are not charged.

Presently, the BLM has identified 14 areas that require more intensive management and special actions to protect their outstanding resources. These areas are called "Special Recreation Management Areas." Distinguishing characteristics of these 14 areas are highlighted in the *Colorado Recreation Opportunity Guide* along with the recreation activities provided by each area. Other areas are being identified through land use planning efforts, so contact your BLM office for the most current listing. Presently, the list includes: Arkansas River, Upper Colorado River, American Flats-Silverton, Gunnison River, Ruby Canyon-Black Ridge, Dolores River, Dominguez Canyon, Powderhorn, Grand Valley, Cochetopa Canyon, Phantom Canyon, North Sand Hills, Thompson Creek, and Piceance Basin. The chart of recreation opportunities indicates that undeveloped camping is allowed on all but one of the 14 "Special Recreation Management Areas."

Many of these 14 areas are quite unique. Did you know that the Black Ridge-Ruby Canyon area has the largest concentration of natural sandstone arches in Colorado? Located near Grand Junction, there is boat access for rafting and canoeing from the north, and access from the south via a four-wheel-drive vehicle. And did you know that the 43,000-acre Powderhorn is a designated primitive area, and provides excellent hiking, hunting, and fishing? The Powderhorn Lakes are renowned for their trout fishing and scenic beauty. Bighorn sheep and elk are also plentiful in the area.

The state is divided into four BLM districts: offices are located in Craig, Grand Junction, Montrose, and Canon City. There are an additional 11 Resource Area offices to assist you in determining if public access exists to the areas you want to use. Maps are available for purchase that show national forests, national parks and monuments, national wildlife refuges, and public lands administered by BLM. For information, contact:

Bureau of Land Management
Colorado State Office
2850 Youngfield Street
Lakewood, CO 80215
(303) 236-2100

SNOW ACTIVITIES

In Colorado, the snows may come well before Thanksgiving or not until Christmas. In a typical year, from November to early April, there is some of the best skiing in the country at more than thirty Colorado areas and resorts; it has a greater number of major ski resorts and areas than any other state. They vary in size from Vail, rated the #1 ski area in America by *SKI Magazine* to Ski Cooper. Colorado has attained an international reputation for its reliable snow conditions. With 300 inches of light, dry snowfall accompanied by 300 days of sunshine, excellent ski lodges and resorts, its no wonder that one-third of the visitors to Colorado each year come for world-class skiing. Most ski areas are located within the national forests in the north-central portion of the state, near Aspen, Vail, and Winter Park.

Colorado offers more than 20,000 acres of skiable terrain for all abilities. Experienced skiers have always found Colorado to be an exciting place to ski, but with 200 miles of beginner trails and over 2,200 professional ski instructors, it's a great place to learn. Colorado boasts 2,200 beginner trails, with more than 60 of them that go all the way from the top of the mountain to the bottom. Keep in mind that most skiers can advance to intermediate slopes

Downhill skiing is by no means the only snow activity in Colorado.

by the third day of lessons. If you are a senior citizen, in the 65 to 69 age group, whether you currently ski or would like to learn, you will receive a discount at most areas; if you are 70, you will ski free. Families are treated to fantastic bargains, and in many cases, children ski free and stay free when accompanied by their parents. Colorado is also one of the pioneers of skiing for the handicapped.

Each season the Colorado Ski Country USA publishes a *Ski Guide* on 28 ski areas that is packed with information including mountain maps, statistics (such as opening and closing dates, types of terrain, etc.), rates, transportation alternatives, accommodations and additional winter activities. Another service of Colorado Ski Country USA is its Airport Reception Centers at Stapleton International Airport in Denver, Walker Field in Grand Junction, and the Colorado Springs Municipal Airport. Updated ski conditions and resort information are available at the booths. For the free guide, and other skiing information, contact:

Colorado Ski Country USA
1560 Broadway, Suite 1440
Denver, CO 80202
(303) 837-0793

Several other important phone numbers are:

Snow Report Line (303) 831-SNOW
Mountain Road Conditions (303) 639-1111
Avalanche Information (303) 236-9435

Downhill skiing is by no means the only snow activity you'll find in Colorado. Cross-country skiing, or ski touring, is becoming increasingly popular. Not only is it a means of escaping the ever-longer lift lines and the cost of lift tickets, but it provides the perfect opportunity to see nature at its best. In recent years, ski resorts have expanded to include extensive cross-country facilities, including lessons, trails, guided tours, and even overnight excursions. There are also several individual cross-country centers located throughout the state. For additional information, contact:

Colorado Cross-Country Ski Association
P.O. Box 1336
Winter Park, CO 80482
(303) 887-2512

In recent years, ski resorts have expanded to include extensive cross-country facilities, including guided tours and overnight excursions.

Many other winter or snow activities exist, such as ice skating, tubing, snowshoeing, sledding, ice fishing, snowcat tours, and snowmobiling. Snowmobiling is an easy-to-learn sport for any age, and is a great way to view Colorado's beautiful alpine meadows. Rentals and tours are available at most Colorado ski resorts. Numerous private outfitters throughout the state offer tours through Colorado's state and national parks and forests. For additional information on snowmobiling, contact:

Colorado Association of Snowmobile Clubs
4784 Weld County Rd. 12
Erie, CO 80416
(303) 654-0867

WILDLIFE

If you are a wildlife enthusiast, whether it be fishing, hunting, or photography, Colorado promises adventure. According to the *Official State Recreation Guide*, Colorado has over 65,000 miles of streams and over 2,000 lakes. Warm-water fishing areas are located primarily on the eastern half of the state and yield catches of yellow perch, bass, northern pike, and walleye, to name a few. In the western half of the state are located the cold-water fishing areas that yield trout, kokanee salmon, and more. Each year, the Colorado Division of Wildlife distributes a booklet entitled *Fishing Season Infor-*

mation for that season. This booklet, distributed free of charge, contains valuable information such as seasons, manner of take, prohibited species, license fees, residency requirements, daily limits, etc.

For general information on fishing, phone (303) 291-7533.

For up-to-date fishing reports, phone (303) 291-7534.

Each fall, Colorado's big game hunting seasons attract sportsmen from all over the world. In fact, Colorado is one of only two states in the country where non-residents can purchase an over-the-counter elk license. Colorado has more elk than any other state. Hunters also pursue deer, bighorn sheep, Rocky Mountain Goat, bobcat, mountain lion, and bear, as well as duck, geese, pheasant, and grouse. Sportsmen can set out on their own or take professionally guided expeditions. Certain big game hunting licenses, unlimited in number, are available prior to the annual season; other limited licenses are available, through application and drawing. Write to the Colorado Division of Wildlife for license fee information and license applications. Hunting information booklets are available; specify species when requesting these free booklets.

For recorded information 24 hours a day, phone:

Big Game Hunting (303) 291-7529
Small Game (303) 291-7546
Game Birds (303) 291-7547
Waterfowl (303) 291-7548

Evidently these youngsters are heading for some fishing adventure where the stream is deeper and wider.

Colorado Division of Parks and Outdoor Recreation

Colorado has more than 250 state wildlife areas for enjoying the very popular, but largely unrecognized pastime of wildlife watching.

If you neither hunt nor fish, you are probably a candidate for Colorado's Watchable Wildlife program. Every time you catch a glimpse of Colorado's abundant wildlife, you are taking part in a very popular but largely unrecognized pastime—wildlife watching. Literally hundreds of thousands of people spend countless hours, watching, photographing, and otherwise observing Colorado's rich wildlife heritage. Colorado has over 250 state wildlife areas that are managed by the Division of Wildlife. Most of these properties are suitable for wildlife watching, hunting, fishing, and trapping. Some provide boating, hiking, camping, or other outdoor recreation opportunities. The *Directory of Colorado Division of Wildlife Properties*, distributed free to the public, includes a location map and direction to each property, as well as hunting, fishing, and recreation information.

The three booklets, referred to above, are all available from:

Colorado Division of Wildlife
6060 Broadway
Denver, CO 80216
(303) 297-1192

Another publication that may be of interest to the outdoor enthusiast is the *Natural Resource Recreation Guide to Colorado*. This resource lists natural resource recreation for six agencies: Colorado Division of Parks and Outdoor Recreation, Colorado Division of Wildlife, Bureau of Land Management, U.S. Forest Service, National Park Service, and the U.S. Fish and Wildlife Service. The brochure divides the state into 15 regions, and lists water, land, and winter sports recreation opportunities for back country, walk-in, four-wheel, roaded open country, highway-rural, and developed-urban settings.

J. Gebert

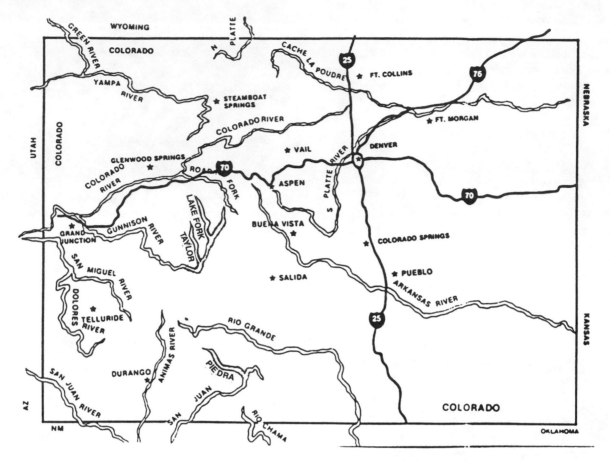

The snowmelt of the Colorado mountains creates challenging rapids in spring and early summer. More than 100 named rivers flow within the boundaries of the state. These rivers offer mountain scenery and access to wild and rugged canyons. Colorado has over 100 river guides and outfitters who lead float trips and whitewater rafting expeditions. River trips range from a couple of hours to a week or more. Rafts are most often used on the Colorado rivers. You can choose from oar-powered trips, where a professional guide does all the work, or from paddle-powered trips, where you paddle with a professional guide calling commands. On some of the rivers, outfitters have canoes and kayaks available; some of the rivers are ideal for float trips for the fishing enthusiast.

The Colorado River Outfitters Association, an association of professional river guides, publishes a brochure that lists various types of trips available through outfitters affiliated with them. Because of the popularity of river running in Colorado, many outfitters require advance reservations. Informa-

Rafts are most often used on the Colorado rivers; some are oar-powered by a professional guide, while others are paddle-powered.

tion provided in the brochure should prove helpful in planning a trip on any of the following rivers: Animas, Arkansas, Blue, Colorado, Dolores, Eagle, Green, Gunnison, Lake Fork, North Platte, Piedra, Poudre, Rio Chama, Rio Grande, Roaring Fork, San

Juan, San Miguel, Taylor, and Yampa rivers. For more information contact:

Colorado River Outfitters Association
P.O. Box 1162
Buena Vista, CO 81211
(303) 333-7831

Their brochure states that "whether you choose whitewater or quietwater, a kayak or a raft, a day trip or a week, a safe trip with the professional members of the Colorado River Outfitters Association will leave you suntanned, excited, and filled with good stories."

Camping Equipment Checklist

The following checklists are designed to guide you in planning your next camping trip. Your needs will vary according to the type, length, and destination of your trip, as well as personal preferences, number of persons included, season of the year, and budget limitations.

Obviously, all items on the checklists aren't needed on any one trip. Since using checklists helps you think more methodically in planning, these extensive lists should serve merely as a reminder of items you may need.

When using these checklists to plan a trip, the item may be checked (✔) if it needs to be taken. Upon returning, if the item was considered unnecessary, a slash could be used: ✗. If a needed item was forgotten, a zero could be used (0); if the item has been depleted and needs to be replenished, an encircling of the check could be used; (✓). This is of particular importance if you camp regularly and keep a camping box packed with staples that can be ready to go on a moment's notice.

Cooking equipment needs are quite dependent on the menu—whether you plan to cook and eat three balanced meals a day or whether you plan to eat non-cooked meals or snacks the entire trip. Many campers find it helpful to jot down the proposed menu for each meal on a 4″ × 6″ index card to help determine the grocery list as well as the equipment needed to prepare the meal. By planning this way, you'll avoid taking equipment you'll never use and you won't forget important items.

Typical Menu with Grocery and Equipment Needs

MEAL: Saturday breakfast		Number of Persons: 5
MENU	GROCERY LIST	EQUIPMENT
orange juice	Tang	camp stove
bacon	10 slices bacon	gasoline, funnel
eggs (scrambled)	8 eggs	folding oven
biscuits	1 can biscuits	frying pan
	peach jelly	baking pan
	honey	pitcher
	margarine	mixing bowl
	salt	cooking fork, spoon
	pepper	

Shelter/Sleeping:
___ Air mattresses
___ Air mattress pump
___ Cots, folding
___ Cot pads
___ Ground cloth
___ Hammock
___ Mosquito netting
___ Sleeping bag or bed roll
___ Tarps (plastic & canvas)
___ Tent
___ Tent stakes, poles, guy ropes
___ Tent repair kit
___ Whisk broom

Extra Comfort:
___ Camp stool
___ Catalytic heater
___ Folding chairs
___ Folding table
___ Fuel for lantern & heater
___ Funnel
___ Lantern
___ Mantels for lantern
___ Toilet, portable
___ Toilet chemicals
___ Toilet bags
___ Wash basin

Clothing/Personal Gear:
___ Bathing suit
___ Boots, hiking & rain
___ Cap/hat
___ Facial tissues
___ Flashlight (small), batteries
___ Jacket/windbreaker
___ Jeans/trousers
___ Pajamas
___ Pocket knife
___ Poncho
___ Prescription drugs
___ Rain suit
___ Sheath knife
___ Shirts
___ Shoes
___ Shorts
___ Socks
___ Sweat shirt/sweater
___ Thongs (for showering)
___ Toilet articles (comb, soap, shaving equipment, toothbrush, toothpaste, mirror, etc.)
___ Toilet paper
___ Towels
___ Underwear
___ Washcloth

Safety/Health:
___ First-aid kit
___ First-aid manual
___ Fire extinguisher
___ Insect bite remedy
___ Insect repellant
___ Insect spray/bomb
___ Poison ivy lotion
___ Safety pins
___ Sewing repair kit
___ Scissors
___ Snake bite kit
___ Sunburn lotion
___ Suntan cream
___ Water purifier

Optional:
___ Binoculars
___ Camera, film, tripod, light meter
___ Canteen
___ Compass
___ Fishing tackle
___ Frisbee, horseshoes, washers, etc.
___ Games for car travel & rainy day
___ Hobby equipment

___ Identification books: birds, flowers, rocks, stars, trees, etc.
___ Knapsack/day pack for hikes
___ Magnifying glass
___ Map of area
___ Notebook & pencil
___ Sunglasses

Miscellaneous:
___ Bucket/pail
___ Candles
___ Clothesline
___ Clothespins
___ Electrical extension cord
___ Flashlight (large), batteries
___ Hammer
___ Hand axe/hatchet
___ Nails
___ Newspapers
___ Pliers
___ Rope
___ Saw, bow or folding
___ Sharpening stone/file
___ Shovel
___ Tape, masking or plastic
___ Twine/cord
___ Wire
___ Work gloves

Cooking Equipment Checklist

**Food Preparation/
Serving/Storing:**

___ Aluminum foil
___ Bags (large & small,
plastic & paper)
___ Bottle/juice can opener
___ Bowls, nested with lids for
mixing, serving & storing
___ Can opener
___ Colander
___ Fork, long-handled
___ Ice chest
___ Ice pick
___ Knife, large
___ Knife, paring
___ Ladle for soups & stews
___ Measuring cup
___ Measuring spoon
___ Pancake turner
___ Potato & carrot peeler
___ Recipes

___ Rotary beater
___ Spatula
___ Spoon, large
___ Tongs
___ Towels, paper
___ Water jug
___ Wax paper/plastic wrap

Cooking:

___ Baking pans
___ Charcoal
___ Charcoal grill (hibachi or
small collapsible type)
___ Charcoal lighter
___ Coffee pot
___ Cook kit, nested/pots &
pans with lids
___ Fuel for stove (gas-
oline/kerosene/liquid
propane)

___ Griddle
___ Hot pads/asbestos gloves
___ Matches
Ovens for baking:
___ Cast iron dutch oven
___ Folding oven for fuel
stoves
___ Reflector oven
___ Tote oven
___ Skewers
___ Skillet with cover
___ Stove, portable
___ Toaster (folding camp
type)
___ Wire grill for open fire

Eating:

___ Bowls for cereal, salad,
soup
___ Cups, paper
___ Forks

___ Glasses, plastic
___ Knives
___ Napkins, paper
___ Pitcher, plastic
___ Plates (plastic, aluminum,
paper)
___ Spoons
___ Table cloth, plastic

___ _____
___ _____

Clean-Up:

___ Detergent (Bio-degrad-
able soap)
___ Dish pan
___ Dish rag
___ Dish towels
___ Scouring pad
___ Scouring powder
___ Sponge

*When it comes to camping equipment, there is a definite dif-
ference between what you pack into the high country . . .*

. . . and what you carry in your travel trailer.

Hiking/Backpacking Checklist

This list is not meant to be all inclusive or necessary for each
trip. It is a guide in choosing the proper gear. Although this list
was prepared for the hiker/backpacker, it is quite appropriate for
anyone using the backcountry, whether they are traveling by
foot, canoe, bicycle, or horse. Parentheses indicate those optional
items that you may not want to carry depending upon the length
of the trip, weather conditions, personal preferences, or necessity.

Ten Essentials for Any Trip:

___ Map
___ Compass
___ First-aid kit
___ Pocket knife
___ Signaling device
___ Extra clothing
___ Extra food
___ Small flashlight/extra
bulb & batteries
___ Fire starter/candle/
waterproof matches
___ Sunglasses

Day Trip (add to the above):

___ Comfortable boots or
walking shoes
___ Rain parka or 60/40
parka

___ Day pack
___ Water bottle/canteen
___ Cup
___ Water purification tablets
___ Insect repellant
___ Sun lotion
___ Chapstick
___ Food
___ Brimmed hat
___ (Guide book)
___ Toilet paper & trowel
___ (Camera & film)
___ (Binoculars)
___ (Book)
___ Wallet & I.D.
___ Car key & coins for
phone
___ Moleskin for blisters
___ Whistle

Overnight or Longer Trips
(add the following):

___ Backpack
___ Sleeping bag
___ Foam pad
___ (Tent)
___ (Bivouac cover)
___ (Ground cloth/poncho)
___ Stove
___ Extra fuel
___ Cooking pot(s)
___ Pot scrubber
___ Spoon (knife & fork)
___ (Extra cup/bowl)
___ Extra socks
___ Extra shirt(s)
___ Extra pants/shorts
___ Extra underwear
___ Wool shirt/sweater
___ (Camp shoes)

___ Bandana
___ (Gloves)
___ (Extra water container)
___ Nylon cord
___ Extra matches
___ Soap
___ Toothbrush/powder/floss
___ Mirror
___ Medicines
___ (Snake bite kit)
___ (Notebook & pencil)
___ Licenses & permits
___ (Playing cards)
___ (Zip-lock bags)
___ (Rip stop repair tape)
___ Repair kit—wire, rivets,
pins, buttons, thread,
needle, boot strings

Region 1

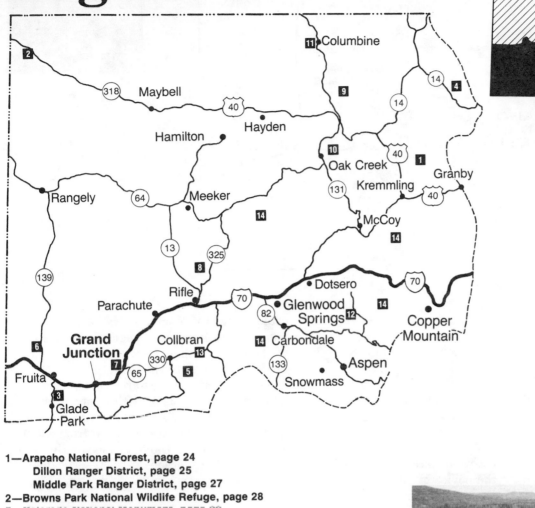

Arapaho National Forest

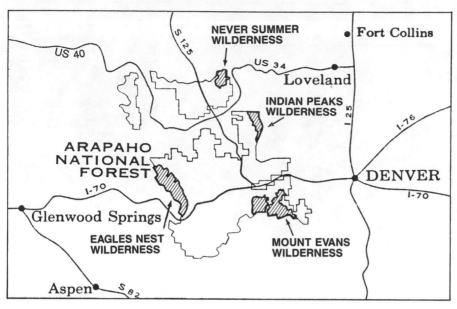

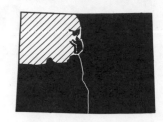

Wilderness Areas

Eagles Nest Wilderness encompasses 133,688 acres on the White River and Arapaho National Forests. Elevations within the wilderness range from 7,850 to 13,534 feet. Over 100 miles of constructed trails are available. Most of the area presents a mental and physical challenge to the advanced hiker. Several other areas in the White River and Arapaho National Forests are better suited for the novice hiker.

Never Summer Wilderness is bordered on the east side by the Never Summer Mountains, ranging in elevation from 8,900 to 12,524 feet. Spruce, fir, and lodgepole pine are abundant at lower elevations. This area contains 7,800 acres and provides a scenic backdrop for Trail Ridge Road.

Mount Evans Wilderness is located about 40 miles southwest of Denver. The Mt. Evans Highway forms a non-wilderness corridor into the center of this 70,000-acre wilderness. Elevations range from 8,400 feet to 14,264-foot Mount Evans. Vegetation at higher elevations consists of alpine treeless plains. Significant stands of spruce fir and lodgepole pine lie below timberline. The wilderness contains the 5,880-acre Abyss Lake Scenic Area, a glacier-carved basin with outstanding scenery.

Indian Peaks Wilderness is located primarily within the Arapaho and Roosevelt national forests although the northernmost portion is lo-cated in Rocky Mountain National Park. The name Indian Peaks was selected because many of the peaks within the wilderness are named for Indian tribes in the West. The 73,391-acre wilderness contains vast areas of alpine tundra, numerous cirque basins with remnant glaciers, and nearly 50 lakes in the shadows of the Continental Divide. Elevations range from 8,400 to 13,000 feet. This is the most frequently visited wilderness in Colorado.

Location

The Arapaho National Forest includes land on both sides of the Continental Divide, which separates the Platte River watersheds that flow to the Atlantic Ocean and the Colorado River watersheds that flow to the Pacific Ocean. Established July 1, 1908 by President Theodore Roosevelt, the 1,025,077-acre forest is named after the plains Indian tribe that frequented the region for summer hunting. The area includes the summit drive to Mount Evans, the highest paved highway in the United States along with 4 wilderness areas.

For Information

Arapaho and Roosevelt
  National Forest Headquarters
240 West Prospect Road
Fort Collins, CO 80526
(303) 498-1100

Dillon Ranger District

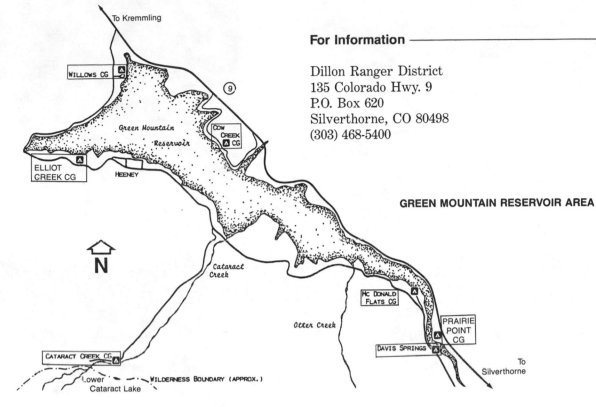

To Kremmling

WILLOWS CG

Green Mountain Reservoir

COW CREEK CG

ELLIOT CREEK CG

HEENEY

N

Cataract Creek

Otter Creek

MC DONALD FLATS CG

PRAIRIE POINT CG

DAVIS SPRINGS

CATARACT CREEK CG

Lower Cataract Lake

WILDERNESS BOUNDARY (APPROX.)

To Silverthorne

For Information

Dillon Ranger District
135 Colorado Hwy. 9
P.O. Box 620
Silverthorne, CO 80498
(303) 468-5400

GREEN MOUNTAIN RESERVOIR AREA

A view from Rollins Pass, which crosses the Continental Divide at an elevation of 11,671 feet.

Campground Locations

Dillon Reservoir has **4** developed campgrounds (Heaton Bay, Peak One, Pine Cove, & Prospector), 2 group camping areas (Gold Pan & Windy Point), and 3 areas designated for only overnight camping for self-contained units (Blue River Inlet, Giberson Bay, & Snake River Inlet). The reservoir is south of Silverthorne off of US 6 and SH 9 with access from I-70 via Exits 201, 203, and 205.

Blue River is northwest of Silverthorne on SH 9; approximately mid-way between Silverthorne and Green Mountain Reservoir.

McDonald Flats and *Prairie Point* are developed campgrounds on Green Mountain Reservoir; the reservoir is approximately 20 miles northwest of Silverthorne on SH 9, via the I-70 Exit 205.

Cow Creek, Davis Springs, Elliot Creek, and *Willows* are all undeveloped campgrounds located along the shoreline of Green Mountain Reservoir.

Cataract Creek is an undeveloped campground located on Cataract Creek south of Green Mountain Reservoir near Lower Cataract Lake.

Arapaho National Forest   25

Dillon Ranger District *(continued)*

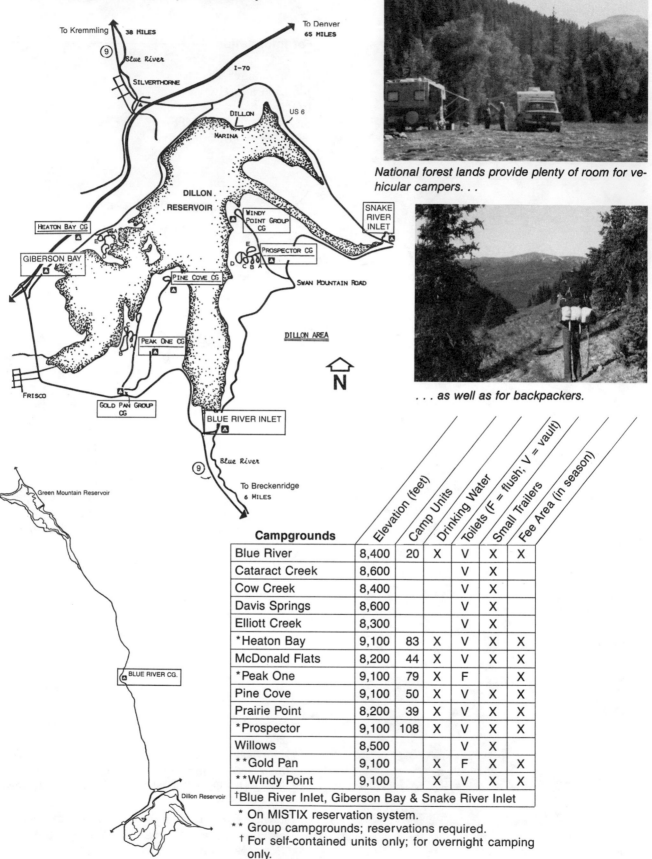

National forest lands provide plenty of room for vehicular campers...

... as well as for backpackers.

Campgrounds	Elevation (feet)	Camp Units	Drinking Water	Toilets (F = flush; V = vault)	Small Trailers	Fee Area (in season)
Blue River	8,400	20	X	V	X	X
Cataract Creek	8,600			V	X	
Cow Creek	8,400			V	X	
Davis Springs	8,600			V	X	
Elliott Creek	8,300			V	X	
*Heaton Bay	9,100	83	X	V	X	X
McDonald Flats	8,200	44	X	V	X	X
*Peak One	9,100	79	X	F		X
Pine Cove	9,100	50	X	V	X	X
Prairie Point	8,200	39	X	V	X	X
*Prospector	9,100	108	X	V	X	X
Willows	8,500			V	X	
**Gold Pan	9,100		X	F	X	X
**Windy Point	9,100		X	V	X	X
†Blue River Inlet, Giberson Bay & Snake River Inlet						

* On MISTIX reservation system.

** Group campgrounds; reservations required.

† For self-contained units only; for overnight camping only.

Middle Park Ranger District

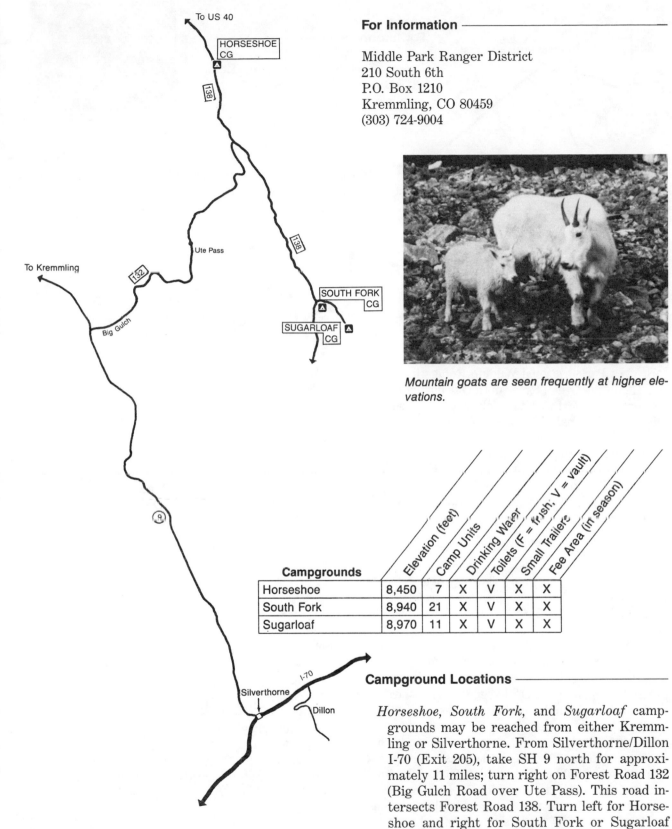

To US 40

HORSESHOE CG

138

138

Ute Pass

To Kremmling

132

Big Gulch

SOUTH FORK CG

SUGARLOAF CG

9

Silverthorne

I-70

Dillon

For Information

Middle Park Ranger District
210 South 6th
P.O. Box 1210
Kremmling, CO 80459
(303) 724-9004

Mountain goats are seen frequently at higher elevations.

Campgrounds	Elevation (feet)	Camp Units	Drinking Water	Toilets (F = fresh, V = vault)	Small Trailers	Fee Area (in season)
Horseshoe	8,450	7	X	V	X	X
South Fork	8,940	21	X	V	X	X
Sugarloaf	8,970	11	X	V	X	X

Campground Locations

Horseshoe, South Fork, and *Sugarloaf* campgrounds may be reached from either Kremmling or Silverthorne. From Silverthorne/Dillon I-70 (Exit 205), take SH 9 north for approximately 11 miles; turn right on Forest Road 132 (Big Gulch Road over Ute Pass). This road intersects Forest Road 138. Turn left for Horseshoe and right for South Fork or Sugarloaf campgrounds.

Browns Park National Wildlife Refuge

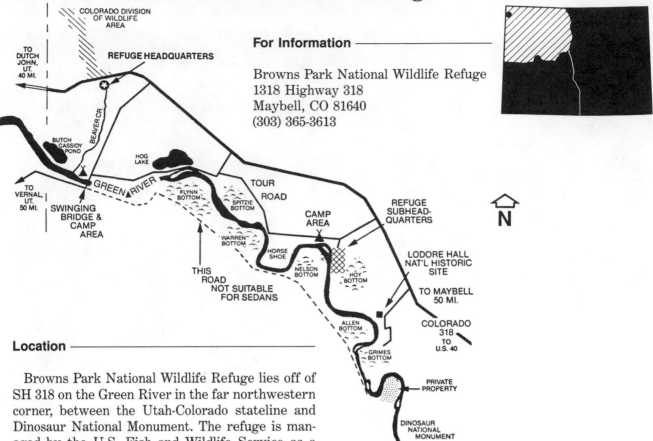

TO DUTCH JOHN, UT. 40 MI.

REFUGE HEADQUARTERS

BEAVER CR.

BUTCH CASSIDY POND

HOG LAKE

GREEN RIVER

TO VERNAL, UT. 50 MI.

SWINGING BRIDGE & CAMP AREA

FLYNN BOTTOM

SPITZIE BOTTOM

WARREN BOTTOM

HORSE SHOE

NELSON BOTTOM

THIS ROAD NOT SUITABLE FOR SEDANS

TOUR ROAD

CAMP AREA

HOY BOTTOM

REFUGE SUBHEAD-QUARTERS

LODORE HALL NAT'L HISTORIC SITE

TO MAYBELL 50 MI.

COLORADO 318 TO U.S. 40

ALLEN BOTTOM

GRIMES BOTTOM

PRIVATE PROPERTY

DINOSAUR NATIONAL MONUMENT

N

For Information

Browns Park National Wildlife Refuge
1318 Highway 318
Maybell, CO 81640
(303) 365-3613

Location

Browns Park National Wildlife Refuge lies off of SH 318 on the Green River in the far northwestern corner, between the Utah-Colorado stateline and Dinosaur National Monument. The refuge is managed by the U.S. Fish and Wildlife Service as a nesting and resting area for migratory waterfowl. This is remote country. Maybell, Colorado and Vernal, Utah are 50 miles away and Dutch John, Utah is 40 miles. The Browns Park Store is within 5 miles of the refuge.

About the Refuge

In pristine times, annual flooding of the Green River maintained the wet meadows preferred by nesting waterfowl. Flaming Gorge Dam now prevents this flooding. Consequently, refuge personnel now pump water from the river to maintain approximately 6,000 acres of developed waterfowl habitat. This semiarid region receives less than 10 inches of precipitation annually. Ducks, geese, and other water birds travel hundreds of miles to use this unique habitat.

Mallards, redheads, teal, canvasbacks, and other ducks, and Great Basin Canada geese nest on the Refuge. About 300 goslings and 2,500 ducklings are hatched annually. The waterfowl population swells by thousands during the spring and fall migrations. Wading birds, shore birds, song birds, and a variety of hawks and eagles also use the refuge during vari-

ous seasons. Resident species include mule deer, antelope, chukar partridge, and sage grouse. Elk and bighorn sheep occasionally visit the refuge. Hikers, sightseers, and photographers are welcome year-round. A graveled tour road provides ample opportunities to view wildlife and wildlife habitat.

Facilities & Activities

primitive camping ONLY
  15 sites at Swinging Bridge
  20 sites at Crook
restrooms (only facility)
NO water
NO fee
picnicking
Refuge Headquarters
auto tour (gravel road)
refuge leaflet
species list
boating on Butch Cassidy Pond (non-motorized)
boating on Green River (motorized)
fishing
hunting
hiking

Colorado National Monument

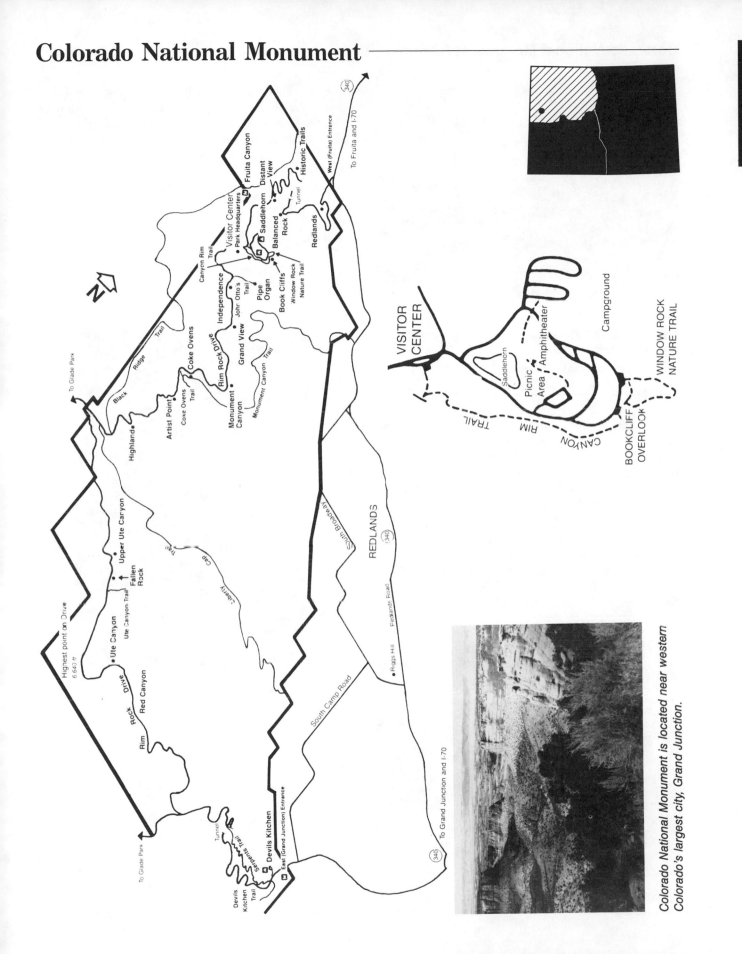

VISITOR CENTER

Saddlehorn

Picnic Area

Amphitheater

Campground

CANYON RIM TRAIL

BOOKCLIFF OVERLOOK

WINDOW ROCK NATURE TRAIL

Fruita Canyon
Distant View
Historic Trails
West (Fruita) Entrance
To Fruita and I-70

Visitor Center
Park Headquarters
Saddlehorn
Balanced Rock
Tunnel
Redlands

Canyon Rim Trail
Independence
John Otto's
Grand View
Pipe Organ
Book Cliffs
Window Rock Nature Trail

Rim Rock Drive
Coke Ovens
Coke Ovens Trail
Monument Canyon
Monument Canyon Trail

Black Ridge Trail

Artist Point

Highland

To Glade Park

N

Highest point on Drive 6,640 ft

Upper Ute Canyon
Fallen Rock

Ute Canyon
Ute Canyon Trail

Liberty Cap Trail

Rim Rock Drive
Red Canyon

Tunnel
Serpents Trail

Devils Kitchen Trail
Devils Kitchen
East (Grand Junction) Entrance

To Glade Park

South Camp Road

REDLANDS

South Broadway

Federlands Road

Riggs Hill

To Grand Junction and I-70

340

Colorado National Monument is located near western Colorado's largest city, Grand Junction.

Colorado National Monument (continued)

Many of the red sandstone monoliths are visible from overlooks along the 23-mile-long Rim Rock Drive.

Location

Colorado National Monument, open year-round, is south of I-70 between Fruita and Grand Junction. A 35-mile circuit can be made from Grand Junction or Fruita across the park on Rim Rock Drive and then back to your point of origin via SH 340. To reach the west entrance of the park, take Exit 19 at Fruita, and travel south on SH 340. The Visitor Center and Saddlehorn Campground are located just 4 miles from the west entrance on Rim Rock Drive. To reach the east entrance of the park, from I-70 in Grand Junction, take US 50 south to SH 340, then right on Rim Rock Drive. The 20,450-acre park

Hiking into the canyon is also a good way to see this geologic wonder.

displays sheer-walled canyons, towering monoliths, and strange formations that reflect the action of time and weather on colorful sandstone. Hiking on one of the many trails along the canyon rim or into the canyon is a good way to see the monument. Elevation: 5,700 feet at Saddlehorn Campground.

For Information

Colorado National Monument
Fruita, CO 81521
(303) 858-3617

The area was proclaimed a national monument in 1911.

Facilities & Activities

80 campsites (no reservations)
camping fees collected during the summer only
picnic areas
over 30 miles of constructed nature/hiking trails
backcountry camping for hikers and horseback riders (obtain a free permit at the visitor center)
Visitor Center exhibits and audiovisual program
seasonal interpretive talks and campfire programs
auto tour on Rim Rock Drive, with numerous overlooks

Colorado State Forest

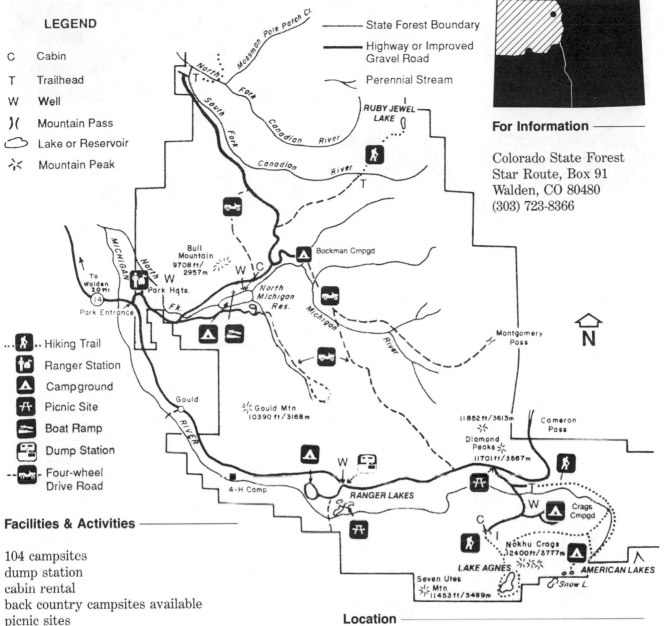

LEGEND

C   Cabin

T   Trailhead

W   **Well**

)(Mountain Pass

⌒   Lake or Reservoir

⁂   Mountain Peak

——— State Forest Boundary

━━━ Highway or Improved Gravel Road

～ Perennial Stream

Hiking Trail

Ranger Station

Campground

Picnic Site

Boat Ramp

Dump Station

Four-wheel Drive Road

For Information

Colorado State Forest
Star Route, Box 91
Walden, CO 80480
(303) 723-8366

RUBY JEWEL LAKE

Bockman Cmpgd

Bull Mountain 9708 ft/ 2957m

To Walden 20 mi

Park Hqts.

Park Entrance

North Michigan Res.

Montgomery Pass

N

Gould

Gould Mtn 10390 ft/3168m

Cameron Pass

11852 ft/3613m

Diamond Peaks 11701 ft/3567m

4-H Camp

RANGER LAKES

Crags Cmpgd

Nokhu Crags 12400ft/3777m

LAKE AGNES

AMERICAN LAKES

Snow L.

Seven Utes Mtn 11453 ft/3489m

Facilities & Activities

104 campsites
dump station
cabin rental
back country campsites available
picnic sites
boating (wakeless; special restrictions)
boat ramps
fishing
snowmobiling
cross-country skiing
ice skating
ice fishing
snow tubing
winter camping
50 miles of hiking trails
112 miles of bicycling trails
112 miles of horseback trails
stables/horse rental
75 miles of 4-wheel drive trails

Location

Colorado State Forest is located on SH 14, 75 miles west of Ft. Collins over Cameron Pass, and southeast of Walden. The state forest is high country, ranging in elevation from 8,500 to 12,500 feet, so visitors may find they need time to acclimate. Until mid-summer, mosquito repellant is a necessity. The park stretches along the west side of the Medicine Bow Mountains and into the north end of the Never Summer Range. The 70,708 acres include 50,000 acres of backcountry suitable for hiking, backpacking, horseback riding, and four-wheeling. Several lakes, totaling 130 surface acres, provide opportunities for lake and stream fishing.

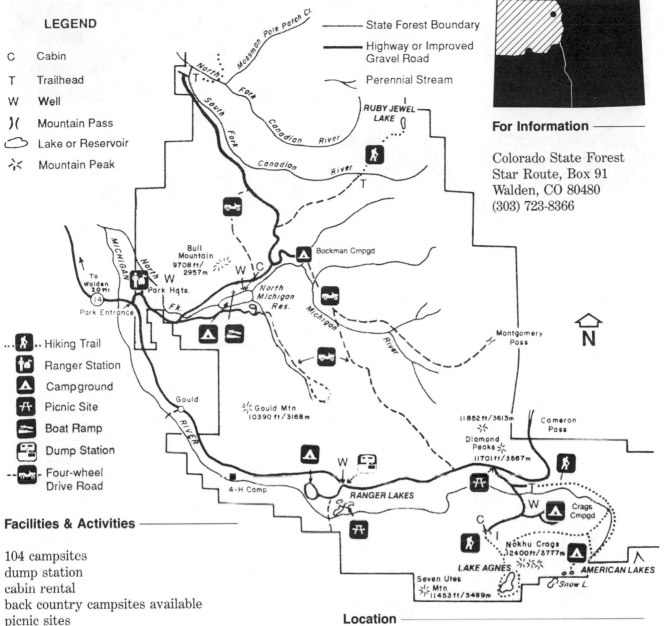

Grand Mesa National Forest

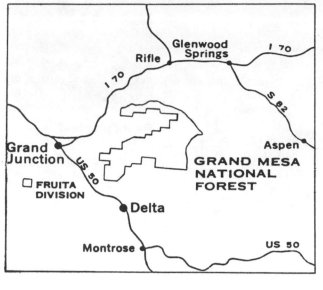

Location

Grand Mesa National Forest is located south of I-70, which runs from Denver to Grand Junction, and is bounded by White River National Forest on the north and northeast and Gunnison National Forest on the east. Grand Mesa has stands of aspen and 250 lakes and reservoirs atop a mesa. The Gunnison, Grand Mesa, and Uncompahgre national forests were administratively combined in 1976.

For Information

Grand Mesa-Uncompahgre and Gunnison
  National Forests Headquarters
2250 Highway 50
Delta, CO 81416
(303) 874-7691

Collbran Ranger District

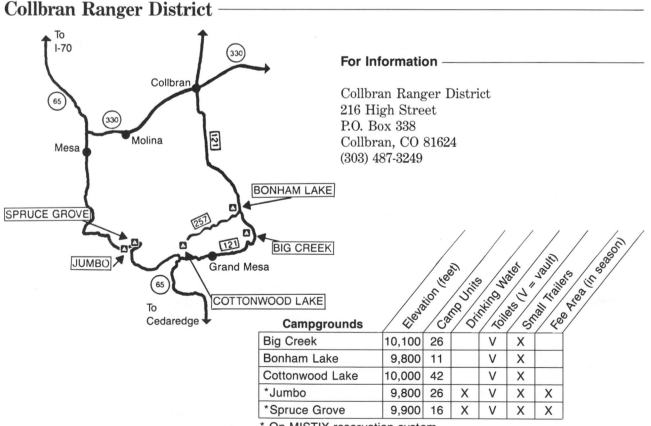

For Information

Collbran Ranger District
216 High Street
P.O. Box 338
Collbran, CO 81624
(303) 487-3249

Campgrounds	Elevation (feet)	Camp Units	Drinking Water	Toilets (V = vault)	Small Trailers	Fee Area (in season)
Big Creek	10,100	26		V	X	
Bonham Lake	9,800	11		V	X	
Cottonwood Lake	10,000	42		V	X	
*Jumbo	9,800	26	X	V	X	X
*Spruce Grove	9,900	16	X	V	X	X

* On MISTIX reservation system.

Collbran Ranger District *(continued)*

Campground Locations

Big Creek—from SH 330 at Collbran, travel 15 miles south on Forest Road 121; then 1 mile west on Forest Road 121A past the Big Creek Reservoir.

Bonham Lake—from SH 330 at Collbran, travel 12 miles south on Forest Road 121; then ¹⁄₁₀ mile west on Forest Road 257 to Bonham Reservoir.

Cottonwood Lake—from SH 330 at Collbran, travel 12 miles south on Forest Road 121; then 4 miles west on Forest Road 257.

Jumbo—on SH 65, travel through Mesa and go south for 13 miles; then ¹⁄₁₀ mile south on Forest Road 252.

Spruce Grove—on SH 65, travel through Mesa and go south for 15 miles.

Grand Junction Ranger District

For Information

Grand Junction Ranger District
764 Horizon Drive, Room 115
Grand Junction, CO 81506
(303) 242-8211

Campground Locations

Trickle Park, Twin Lake, and *Weir and Johnson* campgrounds—located within a few miles of each other. From Cedaredge, travel 16 miles north on SH 65; then 8 miles east on Forest Road 121 to reach Trickle Park. To reach Twin Lake, go 1 more mile on Forest Road 121, then east on Forest Road 126 for 2 miles. Weir and Johnson is 1 mile beyond Twin Lake.

Carp Lake, Valley View, and *Ward Lake*—all located 16 miles north of Cedaredge on SH 65 at the Forest Road 121 junction. Carp Lake and Valley View are across the road from one another; Ward Lake is 1 mile east on Forest Road 121.

Four other campgrounds are located farther east on Forest Road 121 from the SH 65 junction:
—*Eggleston Lake* is 3½ miles.
—*Crag Crest* is 4 miles.
—*Fish Hawk* is approximately 5 miles.
—*Kiser Creek* is 3 miles east, then ¹⁄₁₀ mile south on Forest Road 123.

Island Lake and *Little Bear* are reached by traveling 1 mile past the SH 65 and Forest Road 121 junction; then left on Forest Road 116 for less than a mile. Both campgrounds are near Island Lake.

Campgrounds	Elevation (feet)	Camp Units	Drinking Water	Toilets (V = vault)	Small Trailers	Fee Area (in season)
*Carp Lake	10,300	20	X	V	X	X
Crag Crest	10,100	11	X	V	X	X
Eggleston Lake	10,100	6	X	V	X	X
Fish Hawk	10,200	5		V	X	
*Island Lake	10,300	41	X	V	X	X
Kiser Creek	10,100	12		V	X	X
*Little Bear	10,200	36	X	V	X	X
Trickle Park	10,100	5		V	X	
Twin Lake	10,300	13		V	X	
*Valley View	10,200	8	X	V	X	X
*Ward Lake	10,200	27	X	V	X	X
Weir and Johnson	10,500	12		V	X	

* On MISTIX reservation system.

Highline State Recreation Area

Location

Highline State Recreation Area, a city-like park in a rural setting, is located west of Grand Junction and quite close to the Utah border. Take Exit 15 from I-70 and travel north on SH 139 for 6 miles; turn west on Q Road and travel 1.3 miles to 11.8 Road, then north 1 mile to the park entrance. The 570-acre park has 174 surface-acres for boating, fishing, and water skiing on Highline Lake. Only hand- or electric-powered boats are allowed on Mack Mesa Lake, noted for its fine early season trout fishing. Elevation: 4,700 feet.

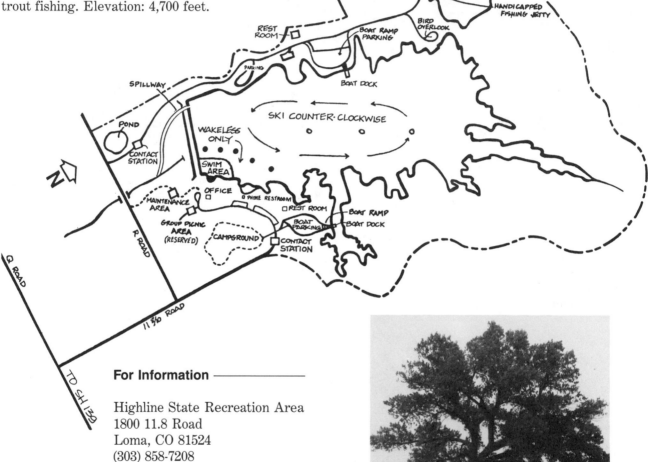

For Information

Highline State Recreation Area
1800 11.8 Road
Loma, CO 81524
(303) 858-7208

Facilities & Activities

25 campsites	fishing
dump station	water skiing
picnic sites	water tubing
group picnic area available	sailboarding
swimming	ice skating
boating (special restrictions)	ice fishing
boat ramps	winter camping

This camping rig at Highline is dwarfed by the size of this magnificent cottonwood tree.

Island Acres State Recreation Area

For Information

Island Acres State Recreation Area
P.O. Box B
Palisade, CO 81526
(303) 464-0548

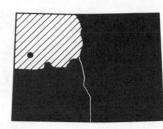

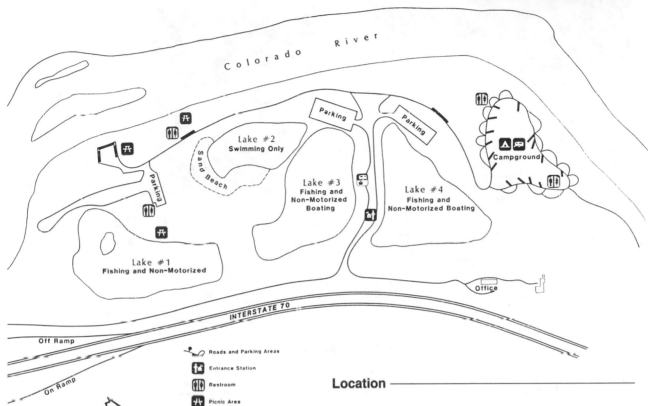

Colorado River

Parking

Parking

Lake #2
Swimming Only

Sand Beach

Lake #3
Fishing and
Non-Motorized
Boating

Lake #4
Fishing and
Non-Motorized Boating

Campground

Parking

Lake #1
Fishing and Non-Motorized

Office

INTERSTATE 70

Off Ramp

On Ramp

N

Roads and Parking Areas
Entrance Station
Restroom
Picnic Area
Sanitary Dump Station

© Copyright 1989 Aquamaps

In yesteryears, the Island Acres area was used as a campsite for trappers, explorers, and Ute Indians.

Location

Island Acres State Recreation Area is located 15 miles east of Grand Junction on I-70 in scenic De-Beque Canyon. Take Exit 47 and turn east onto a frontage road on the north side of the interstate. Located along the bank of the Colorado River, the park has three small lakes for fishing and non-motorized boating and one small lake for swimming only. Picnicking is one of Island Acres' most popular activities at this 130-acre recreation area. Elevation: 4,700 feet.

Facilities & Activities

32 campsites	sailboarding
dump station	cross-country skiing
picnic sites	ice skating
group picnic area available	ice fishing
swimming	winter camping
boating (wakeless)	1 mile of hiking trails
fishing	

Rifle Gap State Recreation Area/Rifle Falls State Park

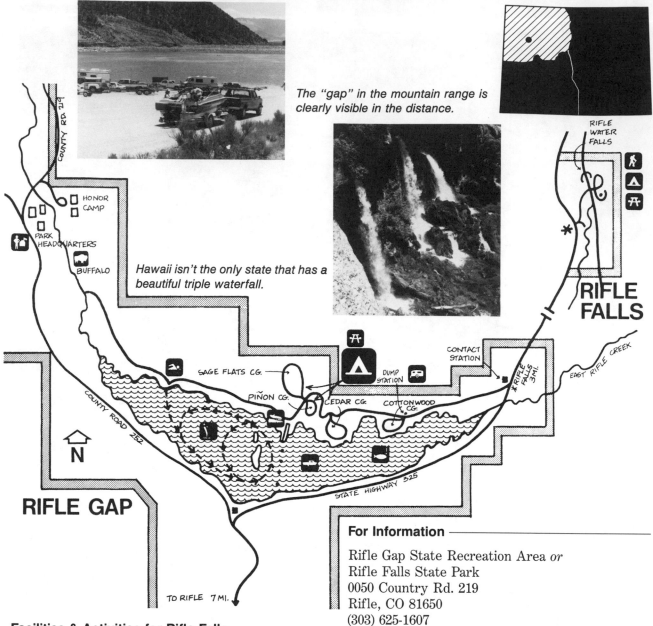

The "gap" in the mountain range is clearly visible in the distance.

Hawaii isn't the only state that has a beautiful triple waterfall.

RIFLE FALLS

RIFLE GAP

TO RIFLE 7 MI.

For Information

Rifle Gap State Recreation Area *or*
Rifle Falls State Park
0050 Country Rd. 219
Rifle, CO 81650
(303) 625-1607

Location

The town of Rifle is located on I-70 between Grand Junction and Glenwood Springs. The parks are north of Rifle and are reached by taking Exit 90 to Rifle from I-70; SH 13 north for 3 miles through Rifle; then SH 325 for 5 miles to Rifle Gap. The clear waters of the 350-acre reservoir at Rifle Gap afford some of Colorado's best scuba diving; this park has an additional 1,484 land acres. Rifle Falls is 5 miles beyond Rifle Gap on SH 325; a much smaller park with just 40 acres, but quite unique with its limestone caves and triple waterfall. Elevation: Rifle Gap—6,000 feet; Rifle Falls—6,600.

Facilities & Activities for Rifle Falls

18 campsites	winter camping
picnic sites	2 miles of hiking trails
fishing	

Facilities & Activities for Rifle Gap

46 campsites	water skiing
dump station	sailboarding
picnic sites	snowmobiling
swimming	cross-country skiing
boating	ice fishing
boat ramps	winter camping
fishing	horseback riding

Routt National Forest

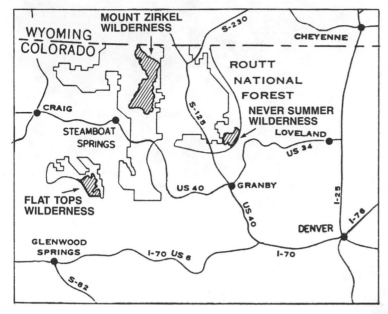

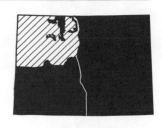

For Information

Routt National Forest Headquarters
29587 West U.S. Highway 40, Suite 20
Steamboat Springs, CO 80487
(303) 879-1722

Location

Routt National Forest includes 1,125,145 acres of federal lands within its boundaries. The Continental Divide and spectacular peaks of the Mt. Zirkel Wilderness split the major watersheds of the National Forest. On the East, the North Park region is drained by the North Platte River, a tributary of the Missouri and Mississippi; on the west, the Yampa River flows to the Green and Colorado. Elevations are high, ranging from 7,000 feet in the irrigated valleys to 13,000 feet along the Divide. Routt National Forest was established by President Theodore Roosevelt in 1905 as the Park Range Reserve. The name was later changed to honor Colonel John N. Routt, the last territorial and the first state governor of Colorado.

Picnic tables and fire rings are provided at most designated campsites.

Trailheads can provide valuable information for trail users.

Special Notes

For summer, expect warm days and cool to freezing nights, especially in the high country. July and August are considered the warmest, and most high mountain lakes are free of ice during this period. The rainy season lasts from mid-July through August; the first snow may occur as early as the first of September. Even with cool weather and high elevations, there are numerous pesky mosquitoes part of the summer. The Routt is known for its abundant and often rare types of wildflowers. There are approximately 231 species of birds and 60 species of mammals as well as over 700 miles of maintained trails on the Routt.

Routt National Forest (continued)

Wilderness Areas

139,818-acre *Mt. Zirkel Wilderness* straddles the Park Range of the Continental Divide. The physiography ranges from spruce-fir to alpine meadow and rock. There are 14 peaks that reach an elevation near 12,000 feet; the highest is Mt. Zirkel with an elevation of 12,180 feet. There are more than 65 lakes, 30 of which are named. Snow persists over most of the area until late June and many snowbanks remain all summer. There are seven relatively easy access points into the Mt. Zirkel Wilderness.

Flat Tops Wilderness contains 235,230 acres on the White River and Routt National Forests. The dominant physical feature is an area known as the White River Plateau—a flattened dome composed of geological strata capped with lava. This great lava cap and sub-strata have eroded to form river canyons and lake beds on the plateau itself. About 160 miles of trails are available for both foot and

This trio of hungry hikers appears quite organized for their lunch break.

horse travel across this high plateau at approximately 10,000 feet elevation.

Never Summer Wilderness contains 7,800 acres on the Arapaho and Routt National Forests and provides a scenic backdrop for Trail Ridge Road. The wilderness is bordered on the east side by the Never Summer Mountains, ranging in elevation from 8,900 to 12,524 feet.

Bears Ears Ranger District

The high plateau of the Routt National Forest offers miles of horse trails.

Campground Locations

Freeman—12 miles north of Craig on SH 13; then 8.5 miles northeast on Forest Road 112-2b (Moffat County Road 11).

Sawmill—11.5 miles north of Craig on SH 13; then approximately 10 miles northeast on Forest Road 110.

For Information

Bears Ears Ranger District
356 Ranney St.
Craig, CO 81625
(303) 824-9438

Campgrounds	Elevation (feet)	Camp Units	Drinking Water	Toilets (V = vault)	Small Trailers	Fee Area (in season)
Freeman	8,800	17	X	V	X	X
Sawmill	9,000	6		V	X	

Hahns Peak Ranger District

Campground Locations

Hahns Peak Lake—25 miles north of Steamboat Springs on County Road 129 (Elk River Road); then 2.5 miles west on Forest Road 486.

Seedhouse and *Hinman* campgrounds—both are located on Forest Road 400 (Seedhouse Road) off of County Road 129 (Elk River Road) 15 miles north of Steamboat Springs. Seedhouse is 9.5 miles northeast on Forest Road 400; Hinman is 6 miles northeast, then ½ mile south on Reed Creek Road 440.

Dry Lake, *Summit Lake*, and *Granite* campgrounds—are all located northeast of Steamboat Springs; take Strawberry Park Road north for 4 miles, then turn right on Buffalo Pass Road (Forest Road 60):

—*Dry Lake* is 3.6 miles east on Buffalo Pass Road.

—*Summit Lake* is 12 miles east.

—*Granite* is 12 miles east, then 5 miles south on Forest Road 310 to Fish Creek Reservoir.

Meadows, *Walton Creek*, and *Dumont Lake*/ Campgrounds—all three are located southeast of Steamboat Springs on US 40:

—*Meadows* is 15 miles

—*Walton Creek* is 17 miles

—*Dumont lake* is 22 miles, then north on old US 40

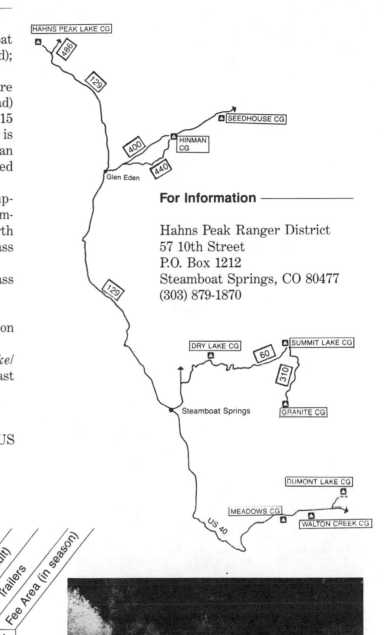

For Information

Hahns Peak Ranger District
57 10th Street
P.O. Box 1212
Steamboat Springs, CO 80477
(303) 879-1870

Campgrounds	Elevation (feet)	Camp Units	Drinking Water	Toilets (V = vault)	Small Trailers	Fee Area (in season)
Dry Lake	8,000	8	X	V	X	X
*Dumont Lake Camp	9,500	22	X	V	X	X
Granite	9,900	6		V		
*Hahns Peak Lake	8,500	26	X	V	X	X
Hinman	7,600	13	X	V	X	X
*Meadows	9,300	30	X	V	X	X
**Seedhouse	8,000	25	X	V	X	X
Summit Lake	10,300	17	X	V	X	X
Walton Creek	9,400	14	X	V	X	X

* On MISTIX reservation system.

** Group camping also available; advanced reservation required.

Living proof that not all campers prefer to cook over an open wood fire.

North Park Ranger District

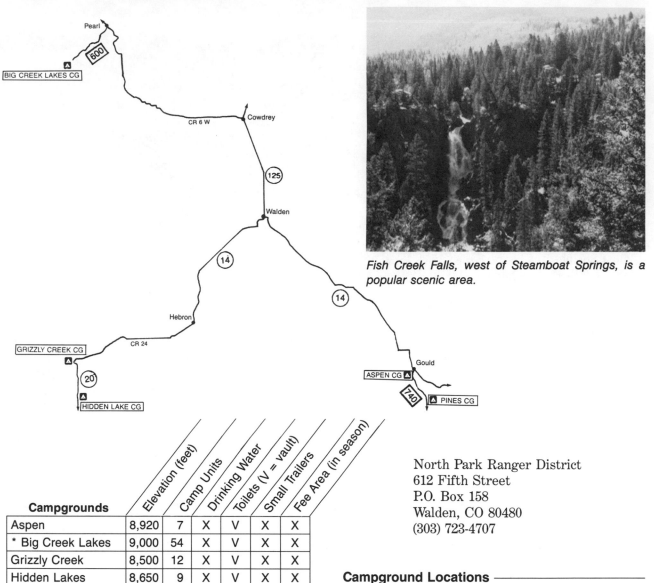

Fish Creek Falls, west of Steamboat Springs, is a popular scenic area.

Campgrounds	Elevation (feet)	Camp Units	Drinking Water	Toilets (V = vault)	Small Trailers	Fee Area (in season)
Aspen	8,920	7	X	V	X	X
* Big Creek Lakes	9,000	54	X	V	X	X
Grizzly Creek	8,500	12	X	V	X	X
Hidden Lakes	8,650	9	X	V	X	X
Pines	9,200	10	X	V	X	X

* On MISTIX reservation system.

North Park Ranger District
612 Fifth Street
P.O. Box 158
Walden, CO 80480
(303) 723-4707

Campground Locations

Big Creek Lakes—take County Road 6W west from Cowdrey, turn left at Pearl on County Road 6A. At forest boundary, follow Forest Road 600 to campground. The campground is 24 miles from services at Cowdrey.

Grizzly Creek and *Hidden Lakes* campgrounds— Take County Road 24 west from SH 14 at Hebron to Forest Road 60. Grizzly Creek is ¼ mile west of forest boundary on Forest Road 60. For Hidden Lakes, go 1 mile beyond Grizzly Creek, turn left on Forest Road 20 and continue south for 4 miles.

Aspen and *Pines* campgrounds—take Forest Road 740 west from Gould. Aspen is the first right after crossing Forest boundary, about 1 mile from Gould; Pines is 4 miles from Gould.

Perhaps he should have borrowed a pack from someone nearer his own size!

Yampa Ranger District

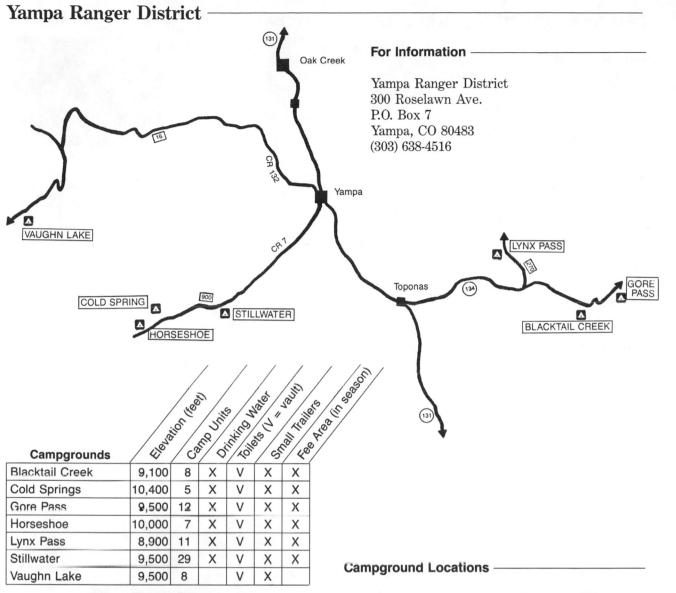

Oak Creek

For Information

Yampa Ranger District
300 Roselawn Ave.
P.O. Box 7
Yampa, CO 80483
(303) 638-4516

Yampa

VAUGHN LAKE

LYNX PASS

GORE PASS

COLD SPRING

STILLWATER

HORSESHOE

Toponas

BLACKTAIL CREEK

Campgrounds	Elevation (feet)	Camp Units	Drinking Water	Toilets (V = vault)	Small Trailers	Fee Area (in season)
Blacktail Creek	9,100	8	X	V	X	X
Cold Springs	10,400	5	X	V	X	X
Gore Pass	9,500	12	X	V	X	X
Horseshoe	10,000	7	X	V	X	X
Lynx Pass	8,900	11	X	V	X	X
Stillwater	9,500	29	X	V	X	X
Vaughn Lake	9,500	8		V	X	

Campground Locations

Vaughn Lake—6 miles northwest of Yampa on County Road 132; then 28.2 miles on Forest Road 16.

Stillwater, *Horseshoe*, and *Cold Springs* campgrounds—are all located southwest of Yampa:
 —Stillwater is 7 miles southwest of Yampa on County Road 7; then 5.9 miles southwest on Forest Road 900.
 —Horseshoe is 2.2 miles beyond Stillwater.
 —Cold Springs is ½ mile beyond Horseshoe.

Lynx Pass, *Blacktail Creek*, and *Gore Pass*—are all located south of Yampa on SH 134 via SH 131:
 —Lynx Pass is 9 miles south of Yampa on SH 131; then 9 miles east on SH 134. Proceed 2.5 miles north on Forest Road 270.
 —Blacktail Creek is 13 miles east on SH 134.
 —Gore Pass is 15½ miles east on SH 134.

This is one of the reasons why so many folks vacation in Colorado!

Stagecoach State Recreation Area

Facilities & Activities

85 campsites
electrical hookups at 27 sites
showers
dump station
picnic sites
group picnic area available
swimming
bathhouse
snackbar
boating
boat ramps
marina
boat rental
fishing
water skiing
sailboarding
cross-country skiing
ice skating
ice fishing
winter camping

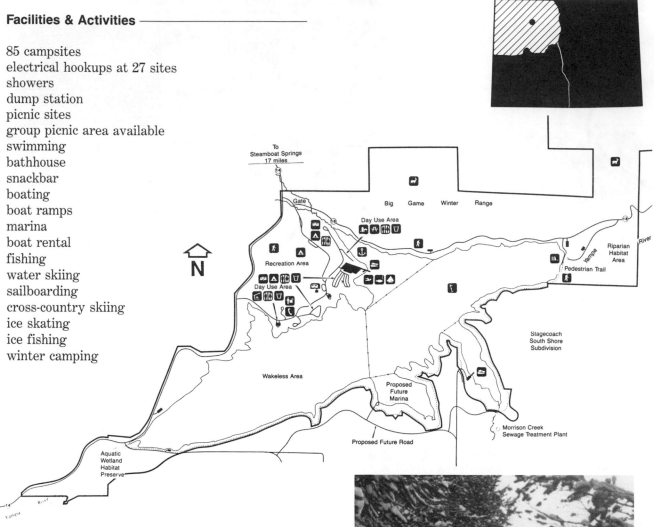

Location

Stagecoach State Recreation Area is situated in the gorgeous Yampa Valley, 4 miles east of the town of Oak Creek. From Steamboat Springs go 4 miles south on US 40, south on SH 131 for 5 miles, then 7 miles south on RCR 14. Surrounded by beautiful rimrock formations, Stagecoach is known for its fascinating history of mining and logging. Many of the reservoir's campgrounds and picnic areas are named after early coal mines and mining camps.

For Information

Stagecoach State Recreation Area
P.O. Box 98
Oak Creek, CO 80467
(303) 736-2436

Traveling uphill on cross-country skis has its difficult moments!

Steamboat Lake State Recreation Area/Pearl Lake State Park

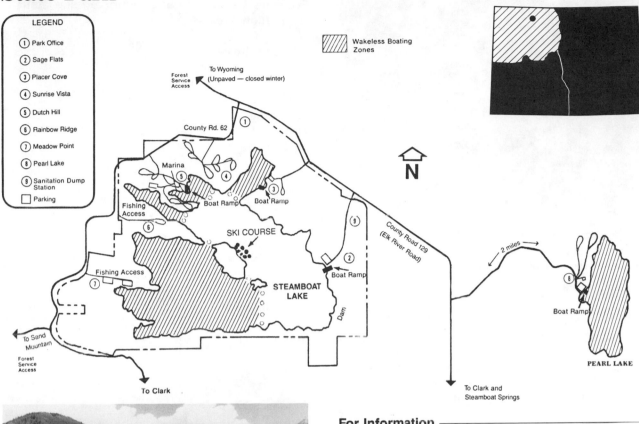

LEGEND

1. Park Office
2. Sage Flats
3. Placer Cove
4. Sunrise Vista
5. Dutch Hill
6. Rainbow Ridge
7. Meadow Point
8. Pearl Lake
9. Sanitation Dump Station
☐ Parking

Wakeless Boating Zones

To Wyoming (Unpaved — closed winter)

Forest Service Access

County Rd. 62

Marina

Boat Ramp

Boat Ramp

Fishing Access

SKI COURSE

Fishing Access

STEAMBOAT LAKE

Dam

County Road 129 (Elk River Road)

To Sand Mountain

Forest Service Access

To Clark

To Clark and Steamboat Springs

2 miles

Boat Ramp

PEARL LAKE

N

Steamboat Lake has three boat ramps. . .

Location

Steamboat Lake State Recreation Area and Pearl Lake State Park, located 27 miles north of Steamboat Springs, are nestled in a valley at the foot of majestic Hahn's Peak, only a few miles west of the Continental Divide. From Steamboat Springs go west for 2 miles on US 40 to County Rd. 129. Turn north; to reach Pearl Lake State Park, go 23 miles to Pearl Lake Road, turn right and go east 2 miles to the park entrance. Steamboat Lake is 3 miles further north on County Rd. 129.

For Information

Steamboat Lake State Recreation Area
Pearl Lake State Park
P.O. Box 750
Clark, CO 80428
(303) 879-3922

. . . resulting in a busy marina.

Judging from the large number of self-contained motor homes in Colorado in the summer, many folks seem to prefer "all the comforts of home" to "roughing it."

About the Parks

These parks are located in one of the most beautiful settings in Colorado, no matter what the season. Two sparkling man-made lakes—Steamboat (1,053 acres) and Pearl (105 acres)—are the principal features. Additional recreational opportunities are provided by the adjacent Routt National Forest. The 169-acre Pearl Lake State Park is known for its quiet and scenic camping and its excellent fly and lure fishing. Steamboat Lake SRA is much larger (1,504 land acres) and has a wide variety of recreational opportunities. Elevation: 8,000 feet.

Steamboat Lake has several wakeless boating zones; these areas are ideal for the rental paddle boats.

Facilities & Activities at Steamboat Lake State Recreation Area

183 campsites
dump station
Visitor/Nature Center
picnic sites
swimming
boating
boat ramps
marina
boat rental
fishing
water skiing
sailboarding
sailboard rental
snowmobiling
cross-country skiing
ice fishing
snow tubing
winter camping
¾ miles of hiking trails

The 105-acre Pearl Lake is designated as a wakeless boating lake.

Facilities & Activities at Pearl Lake State Park

41 campsites
picnic sites
boating (wakeless)
boat ramps
fishing (special restrictions)
snowmobiling
cross-country skiing
ice fishing (special restrictions)
horseback riding

Eleven Mile State Recreation Area is located at an elevation of 8,600 feet; the campground is set among rocky outcroppings (see page 77).

Switchbacks make the trail longer, but the climb much easier.

Humans aren't the only ones who like to climb Grays Peak, one of Colorado's 54 peaks known as "fourteeners" because they are higher than 14,000 feet.

The trail to Isabelle Glacier, in the Roosevelt National Forest, passes by Long Lake.

The 105-acre lake at Pearl Lake State Park is where cutthroat trout dwell and where only fly and lure fishing is permitted (see page 51).

Cross-country skiing provides the perfect opportunity to see nature at its best.

Colorado has more than 65,000 miles of streams and more than 2,000 lakes open for public fishing.

The view from the hiking trail at the Alpine Visitor Center on Trail Ridge Road attests to the fact that one-third of Rocky Mountain National Park is above the tree line (see page 94).

Nestled at the foot of beautiful wooded mountains, Sylvan Lake State Park is a haven for campers and those who take their fishing seriously (see page 53).

Happy Hikers! A blue sky, a good trail, and a pack on their backs!

Curecanti National Recreation Area encompasses the 20-mile long Blue Mesa Lake; when full, it is the largest lake in Colorado (see page 120).

Most of the cliff dwellings of the Anasazi were built at Mesa Verde in the 13th century; three major cliff dwellings are open for visits and many others are visible from Ruins Road.

Most of Colorado's ski areas are located within the national forests in the north-central portion of the state, near Aspen, Vail and Winter Park.

Wheeler Geologic Area consists of spires, domes, and other unusual formations of volcanic tuff. Located in Rio Grande National Forest east of Creede, the area is accessible only via horseback, hiking trails, and a seasonal 4-wheel drive road (see page 135).

Colorado National Monument's colorful sheer-walled canyons and towering monoliths may be conveniently viewed from Rim Rock Drive (see page 29).

Many of the scenic highways in Colorado follow the course of a river.

Curecanti National Recreation Area has two marinas on Blue Mesa Lake: one at Lake Fork Information Center and one at Elk Creek Visitor Center (see page 120).

The fishing must be good here— whether you sit, stand, or fish from a canoe!

49

Mancos State Recreation Area, located only 10 miles from historic Mesa Verde National Monument, is surrounded by the majestic San Juan Mountain range (see pages 128 and 129).

Backpackers on the Continental Divide Trail, north of Wolf Creek Pass.

Camping together is what friends are for!

The 1,450 surface-acre lake at Chatfield State Recreation Area provides room for a variety of water-oriented activities (see page 73).

50

Rocky Mountain National Park is one of the highest regions in the country; 76 named peaks reach elevations of 12,000 feet or higher.

Spectacular Fish Creek Falls, which plunges 283 feet through a geologic fault, is located just west of Steamboat Springs.

No other canyon in North America combines the depth, narrowness, and sheerness of the Black Canyon of the Gunnison.

Summer backpackers often have to cross snow fields; caution should be used!

J. A. Gebert

This camper is surrounded by beautiful alpine scenery, but not by crowds of other campers.

M. Little

Rifle Falls State Park is quite unique with its limestone caves and triple waterfall (see page 36).

J. A. Gebert

Island Acres, located along the bank of the Colorado River, is a unique "clean and green" state recreation area; picnicking is a popular activity (see page 35).

M. Little

Eleven Mile Reservoir is traditionally one of the state's best trout and northern pike fisheries (see page 77).

Sylvan Lake State Park

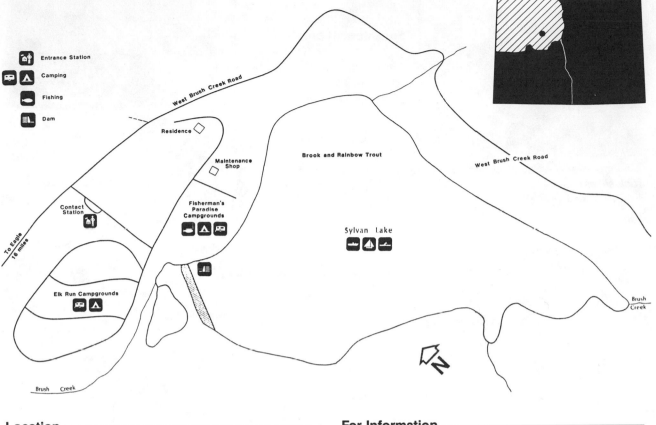

Entrance Station

Camping

Fishing

Dam

West Brush Creek Road

Residence

Maintenance Shop

Brook and Rainbow Trout

West Brush Creek Road

Contact Station

Fisherman's Paradise Campgrounds

To Eagle 18 miles

Sylvan Lake

Elk Run Campgrounds

Brush Creek

Brush Creek

N

Location

Sylvan Lake State Park, nestled at the foot of beautiful, wooded mountains, is located east of Glenwood Springs and south of Eagle. Take Exit 147 from I-70 south through the town of Eagle on Main St., to West Brush Creek Road. Turn right, go south 15 miles to the park entrance. A large portion of the road is unpaved. This 115-acre park, with its 40-acre lake, is said to be a haven for the serious fishing enthusiasts. Elevation 8,500 feet.

Facilities & Activities

51 campsites
picnic sites
boating (wakeless)
boat ramps
fishing
sailboarding
snowmobiling
cross-country skiing
ice fishing
winter camping
1½ miles of hiking trails
horseback riding

For Information

Sylvan Lake State Park
c/o Rifle Gap State Recreation Area
0050 County Rd. 219
Rifle, CO 81650
(303) 625-1607

Sylvan Lake State Park is surrounded by the White River National Forest.

Vega State Recreation Area

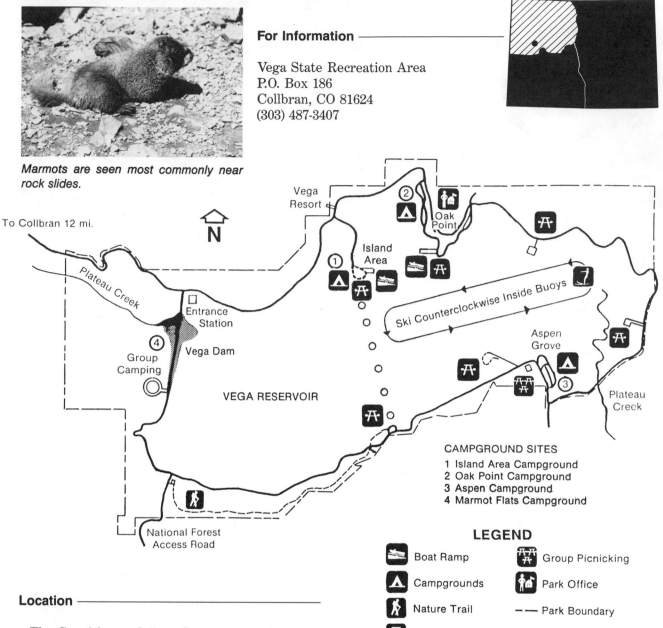

Marmots are seen most commonly near rock slides.

For Information

Vega State Recreation Area
P.O. Box 186
Collbran, CO 81624
(303) 487-3407

To Collbran 12 mi.

Plateau Creek

N

Vega Resort

Island Area

Oak Point

Ski Counterclockwise Inside Buoys

Entrance Station

Vega Dam

Group Camping

VEGA RESERVOIR

Aspen Grove

Plateau Creek

National Forest Access Road

CAMPGROUND SITES
1 Island Area Campground
2 Oak Point Campground
3 Aspen Campground
4 Marmot Flats Campground

LEGEND

Boat Ramp   Group Picnicking

Campgrounds   Park Office

Nature Trail   - - - Park Boundary

Picnic Area

Location

The Spanish word "vega" means meadow, and Vega State Recreation Area was formerly a mountain meadow. In 1962, a 900 surface-acre reservoir was built by the Bureau of Reclamation. Now the meadow is a playground for boaters, water skiers, fishermen, and other outdoor recreationists. To reach the park, take Exit 49 on I-70, go east on SH 65 for 10 miles, continue east for 11 miles on SH 330 to Collbran; then 12 miles to the park entrance. Already well known for its excellent snowmobile system, Vega has subalpine beauty and mild temperatures characteristic of its 8,000-foot altitude. The park, with 898 land acres, provides trail access to Grand Mesa National Forest.

Facilities & Activities

109 campsites	boating
dump station	boat ramps
group campground	fishing
picnic sites	water skiing
group picnic area available	sailboarding
snow tubing	snowmobiling
2 miles of hiking trails	cross-country skiing
2 miles of horseback trails	ice fishing

White River National Forest

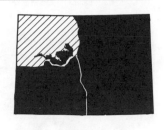

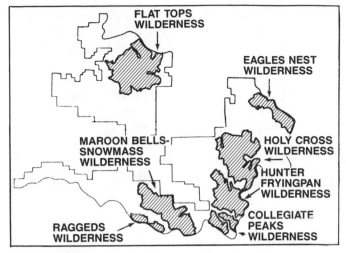

FLAT TOPS
WILDERNESS

EAGLES NEST
WILDERNESS

MAROON BELLS-
SNOWMASS
WILDERNESS

HOLY CROSS
WILDERNESS

HUNTER
FRYINGPAN
WILDERNESS

COLLEGIATE
PEAKS
WILDERNESS

RAGGEDS
WILDERNESS

For Information

White River National Forest Headquarters
9th and Grand
P.O. Box 948
Glenwood Springs, CO 81602
(303) 945-2521

Location

White River National Forest is located in north central Colorado, west of the Continental Divide. With nearly two million acres, the forest contains some of the most spectacular scenery in the Rocky Mountains and is easily accessible from IH 70. One of the largest and oldest national forests in the Rocky Mountains, it was established as a federal timber reserve in 1891 by proclamation of President Benjamin Harrison.

High alpine lakes hold a special beauty for backpackers.

Cross-country skiing, or ski touring, is becoming increasingly popular as a snow activity.

forest environment. The 1,377 miles of maintained trails offer opportunities for many different modes of travel; including hiking, horseback riding, motorbikes, snowmobiles, and cross-country skiing. Wildlife on the forest includes elk, mule deer, black bear, bighorn sheep, mountain goat and mountain lion. There are approximately 20,000 elk, one of the largest herds in North America.

Special Notes

With seven wilderness areas, the White River is one of the most popular national forests in the United States as it offers many opportunities for recreational experiences in a remote and natural

Colorado has over 100 outfitters who lead float trips.

White River National Forest *(continued)*

Stream crossings can pose a real challenge for back-packers.

Wilderness Areas

Collegiate Peaks Wilderness covers 159,900 acres on 3 national forests: Gunnison, White River, and San Isabel. The area contains 8 peaks over 14,000 feet elevation. Climbers should consult reliable guidebooks and seek advice from knowledgeable climbers who are familiar with these peaks. Timberline lakes and high mountain streams offer excellent fishing and scenery.

R. Tatum

To those who listen, water rushing down a rock-strewn river bed makes a melodious sound.

Eagles Nest Wilderness encompasses 133,688 acres on the White River and Arapaho national forests. Elevations within the wilderness range from 7,850 to 13,534 feet. Over 100 miles of constructed trails are available. Most of the area presents a mental and physical challenge to the advanced hiker. Several other areas in the White River and Arapaho national forests are better suited for the novice hiker.

Flat Tops Wilderness encompasses more than 235,000 acres on the White River and Routt na-

tional forests. About 160 miles of trails are available for both foot and horse travel across this high plateau at approximately 10,000 feet elevation.

Holy Cross Wilderness encompasses more than 116,500 acres on the White River and San Isabel national forests. Elevations within the wilderness range from 8,000 to over 13,000 feet. Over 100 miles of constructed trails are available for both foot and horse travel through sometimes rugged terrain.

The view from Capitol Peak of other 14,000-foot peaks in the area is breathtaking, indeed!

Hunter-Fryingpan Wilderness encompasses more than 74,000 acres on the White River National Forest. Elevations within the wilderness range from about 9,000 to over 13,000 feet. Approximately 50 miles of constructed trails are available for both foot and horse travel.

Maroon Bells-Snowmass Wilderness encompasses more than 174,000 acres on the White River and Gunnison national forests. Elevations within the wilderness range from 9,000 to over 14,000 feet. Over 100 miles of constructed trails are available for both foot and horse travel.

Raggeds Wilderness encompasses more than 59,000 acres on the White River and Gunnison national forests. Elevations within the wilderness range from 7,000 to over 13,000 feet. Over 90 miles of constructed trails are available. Weather for the area can vary greatly; but generally, you can expect cool mountain climate with scattered rain showers throughout the summer months. Normally, the Raggeds Wilderness area is snow free from July to September, but conditions depend on the elevation and amount of snowfall each winter.

Aspen Ranger District

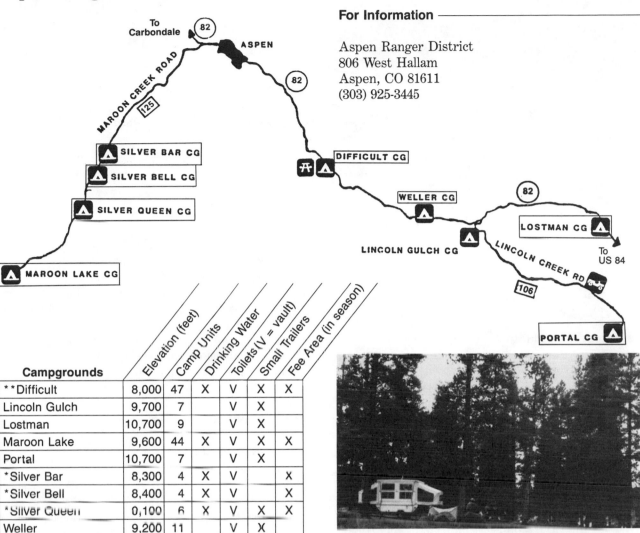

For Information

Aspen Ranger District
806 West Hallam
Aspen, CO 81611
(303) 925-3445

Campgrounds	Elevation (feet)	Camp Units	Drinking Water	Toilets (V = vault)	Small Trailers	Fee Area (in season)
**Difficult	8,000	47	X	V	X	X
Lincoln Gulch	9,700	7		V	X	
Lostman	10,700	9		V	X	
Maroon Lake	9,600	44	X	V	X	X
Portal	10,700	7		V	X	
*Silver Bar	8,300	4	X	V		X
*Silver Bell	8,400	4	X	V		X
*Silver Queen	8,100	6	X	V	X	X
Weller	9,200	11		V	X	

  * On MISTIX reservation system.
 ** Group camping also available; advanced reservation required.

As the shadows lengthen, these skiers are coming down the homestretch of an easy run.

You can always count on lots of trees at the national forest campgrounds.

Campground Locations

Five campgrounds are located southeast of Aspen off of SH 82:
- —*Difficult* is 5 miles southeast of Aspen.
- —*Weller* is 9 miles.
- —*Lincoln Gulch* is 11 miles; then ½ mile on Lincoln Creek Road
- —*Lostman* is 14½ miles.
- —*Portal* is 11 miles; then 7 miles on Lincoln Creek Road (Forest Road 106).

Four campgrounds are located southwest of Aspen on Maroon Creek Road (Forest Road 125):
- —*Silver Bar* is 5 miles southwest of Aspen.
- —*Silver Bell* is 5½ miles.
- —*Silver Queen* is 6½ miles.
- —*Maroon Lake* is 11 miles.

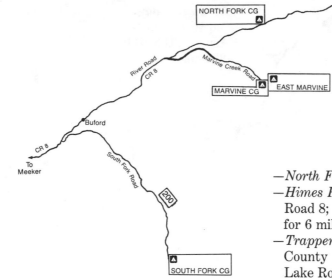

Campground Locations

Six campgrounds are located in the Buford area. Buford is north of Rifle and 17 miles east of Meeker via SH 13 and the River Road (County Road 8):

—*South Fork Campground* is 12 miles southeast on South Fork Road; when traveling from Meeker, turn right on County Road 8 approximately 2½ miles before reaching Buford.

—*East Marvine* and *Marvine* campgrounds are located within a mile of each other and are reached by traveling 8 miles northeast of Buford; then right onto the Marvine Creek Road for approximately 6½ miles.

—*North Fork* is 13 miles northeast of Buford.

—*Himes Peak* is 19 miles from Buford on County Road 8; then right on the Trappers Lake Road for 6 miles to the campground.

—*Trappers Lake* is 19 miles from Buford on County Road 8; then right on the Trappers Lake Road (FR 205) for 10 miles; turn right and cross the bridge just past Trappers Lake Lodge for 1½ miles to any of the 4 campgrounds (Bucks, Cutthroat, Shepherds Rim, & Trapline) in the Trappers Lake Recreation area.

For Information

Blanco Ranger District
361 7th Street
P.O. Box 358
Meeker, CO 81641
(303) 878-4039

Campgrounds	Elevation (feet)	Camp Units	Drinking Water	Toilets (V = vault)	Small Trailers	Fee Area (in season)
East Marvine	8,200	7	X	V	X	X
Himes Peak	9,500	11	X	V	X	X
Marvine	8,200	18	X	V	X	X
*North Fork	8,000	12	X	V	X	X
**North Fork Overflow	8,000	35	X	V	X	X
South Fork	8,000	25	X	V	X	X
Trappers Lake R.A.	9,800	57	X	V	X	X

* Group camping available; reservation required.
** Open only during peak season.

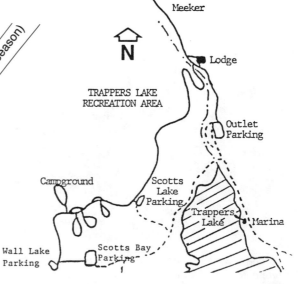

Eagle Ranger District

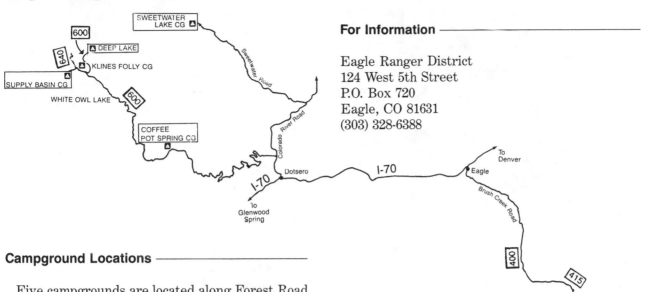

For Information

Eagle Ranger District
124 West 5th Street
P.O. Box 720
Eagle, CO 81631
(303) 328-6388

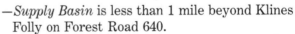

Campground Locations

Five campgrounds are located along Forest Road 600 (Coffee Pot Springs Road), with access from Colorado River Road, 1½ miles north of Dotsero. Dotsero is 14 miles west of Eagle at I-70 Exit 133:

—*Coffee Pot Spring* is approximately 15 miles on Forest Road 600.

—*White Owl Lake* is 26.9 miles; turn left and go 1 mile.

—*Deep Lake* is 29 miles.

—*Klines Folly* is 27.7 miles on Forest Road 600; then left onto Forest Road 640; the first camp-site on left is Klines Folly.

—*Supply Basin* is less than 1 mile beyond Klines Folly on Forest Road 640.

Sweetwater Lake Campground—travel 14 miles west of Eagle on I-70 to the Dotsero Exit 133; then north for 7 miles on the Colorado River Road; turn left onto the Sweetwater Road and go 9 miles; turn left at the lake.

Yoeman Park and *Fulford Cave* campgrounds are located on the same road. From I-70 at Eagle, travel south on Brush Creek Road for 10 miles; then 5.7 miles east on Forest Road 415; Fulford Cave is 1 mile beyond Yoeman Park Campground.

Bridal Veil Falls feeds the incredible Hanging Lake in Glenwood Canyon.

Campgrounds	Elevation (feet)	Camp Units	Drinking Water	Toilets (V = vault)	Small Trailers	Fee Area (in season)
Coffee Pot Spring	10,100	15	X	V	X	
Deep Lake	10,500	21		V	X	
Fulford Cave	9,600	6	X	V		X
Klines Folly	10,200	4		V	X	
Supply Basin	10,200	6		V	X	
Sweetwater Lake	7,700	9	X	V	X	X
White Owl	10,200	5		V	X	
Yoeman Park	9,000	24	X	V	X	X

Holy Cross Ranger District

A spectacular view of Pyramid Peak from the 14,265-foot summit of Castle Peak.

Campground Locations

Five campgrounds are located on US 24 south that goes to Leadville from Exit 171 on I-70 west of Denver:

—*Tigiwon* is approximately 5 miles south, then right onto Forest Road 707 (Tigiwon Road); continue up this dirt road for 6 miles to the campground.

—*Hornsilver* is 12 miles; the campground is on both sides of the highway.

—*Blodgett* is 14 miles, then right on Forest Road 703 (Homestake Road) and proceed ¼ mile to the campground.

—*Gold Park* is 14 miles, then right on Homestake Road and continue down this dirt road for approximately 7 miles. Campground is on the left.

—*Camp Hale* is approximately 17 miles. Enter Camp Hale at the main entrance marked by stone pillars, turn right at the first road and continue to the campground.

Gore Creek—From I-70, take Exit 180 (East Vail); travel southeast and follow the frontage road to the road closure gate, approximately 2 miles. The campground is at the gate.

For Information

Holy Cross Ranger District
401 Main
P.O. Box 190
Minturn, CO 81645
(303) 827-5715

Campgrounds	Elevation (feet)	Camp Units	Drinking Water	Toilets (V = vault)	Small Trailers	Fee Area (in season)
Blodgett	8,900	6	X	V	X	X
*Camp Hale	9,200	21	X	V	X	X
Gold Park	9,300	11	X	V	X	X
Gore Creek	8,700	24	X	V	X	X
Hornsilver	8,800	12	X	V	X	X
**Tigiwon	9,900	9		V	X	

* On MISTIX reservation system.

** Tigiwon Lodge is near campground; it accommodates groups of up to 150 people; reservations required.

Rifle Ranger District

For Information

Rifle Ranger District
0094 County Road 244
Rifle, CO 81650
(303) 625-2371

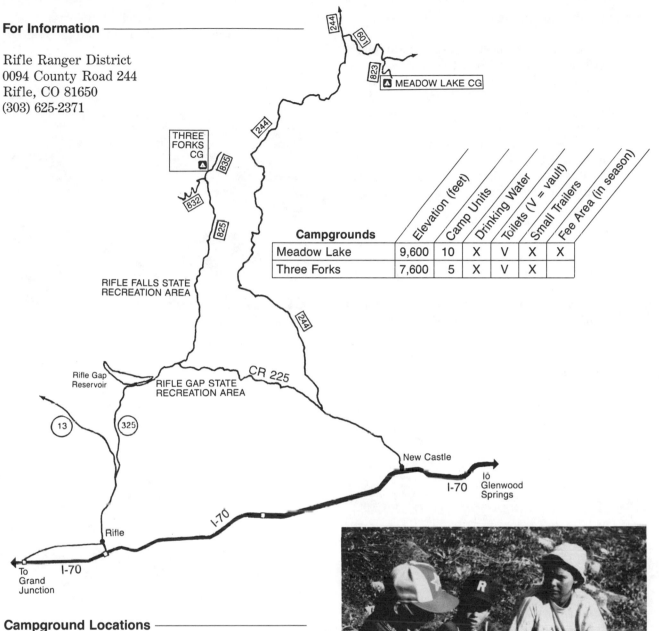

Campgrounds	Elevation (feet)	Camp Units	Drinking Water	Toilets (V = vault)	Small Trailers	Fee Area (in season)
Meadow Lake	9,600	10	X	V	X	X
Three Forks	7,600	5	X	V	X	

Campground Locations

Meadow Lake—Go north of Rifle on SH 13 for 3 miles; turn right on SH 325 for 6½ miles past Rifle Gap Dam. Turn right on County Road 225 for 7 miles; then left on the Buford/New Castle Road (Forest Road 244), continuing for 18 miles to Hiner Springs. Turn right on Forest Road 601 for 3 miles to the turnoff of Forest Road 823 to Meadow Lake.

Three Forks—Go north of Rifle on SH 13 for 3 miles; turn right on SH 325 for 11 miles past Rifle Gap Dam and past Rifle Falls State Park to the White River National Forest. Located at the fork of Forest Roads 825, 832, and 835.

Mountain trails can be rough on the feet; "hot spots" need immediate attention before they develop into blisters.

Sopris Ranger District

Campground Locations

Six campgrounds are located east of Basalt on the Fryingpan Road (Forest Road 105):

—*Little Mattie, Little Maud,* and *Mollie B* campgrounds are all located at Ruedi Reservoir, 16 miles east of Basalt; turn right at the Ruedi Boat Ramp sign.

—*Dearhamer* is 23 miles east of Basalt.

—*Chapman* is 29 miles.

—*Elk Wallow* is 30 miles; turn left at the De-Haven Ranch sign (Forest Road 501) and go 3 miles up the gravel road.

Four campgrounds are located south of Carbondale along SH 133:

—*Janeway* is 11 miles south to the Avalanche Creek turn-off (Forest Road 310); turn left and go ½ mile to the campground.

—*Avalanche* is 11 miles to the Avalanche Creek turn-off; turn left and go 2½ miles on dirt road, staying right when the road forks.

—*Redstone* is 15 miles south; turn left onto bridge and campground is on the left.

—*Bogan Flats* is approximately 22 miles; turn left at the bottom of McClure Pass onto the road to Marble (Forest Road 314); campground is located 1½ miles on left.

Existing fire pits should be used in areas that permit open fires.

Campgrounds	Elevation (feet)	Camp Units	Drinking Water	Toilets (F = flush; V = vault)	Small Trailers	Fee Area (in season)
Avalanche	7,400	13	X	V	X	X
*Bogan Flats	7,600	37	X	V	X	X
*Chapman	8,800	84	X	V	X	X
Dearhamer	7,800	13	X	V	X	X
Elk Wallow	9,000	7		V	X	
Janeway	6,800	10		V	X	
Little Mattie	7,800	20	X	V	X	X
Little Maud	7,800	22	X	F	X	X
*Mollie B	7,800	26	X	F	X	X
Redstone	7,200	24	X	V	X	X

* On MISTIX reservation system.
Bogan Flats & Chapman also have group camping available; reservations are required.

For Information

Sopris Ranger District
620 Main
P.O. Box 309
Carbondale, CO 81623
(303) 963-2266

Region 2

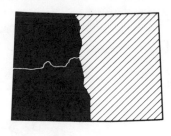

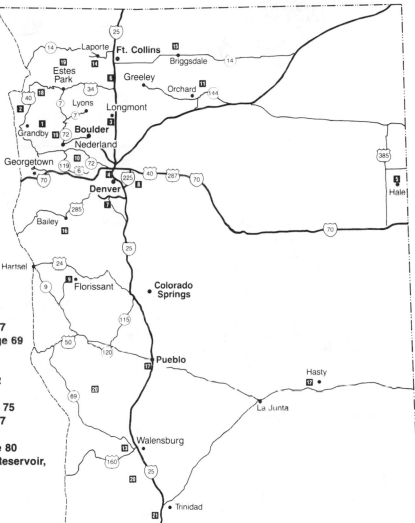

REGION 2

Arapaho National Forest

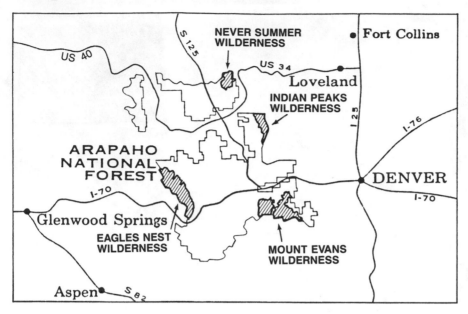

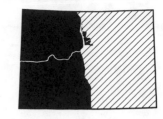

Wilderness Areas

Eagles Nest Wilderness encompasses 133,688 acres on the White River and Arapaho National Forests. Elevations within the wilderness range from 7,850 to 13,534 feet. Over 100 miles of constructed trails are available. Most of the area presents a mental and physical challenge to the advanced hiker. Several other areas in the White River and Arapaho national forests are better suited for the novice hiker.

Never Summer Wilderness is bordered on the east side by the Never Summer Mountains, ranging in elevation from 8,900 to 12,524 feet. Spruce, fir, and lodgepole pine are abundant at lower elevations. This area contains 7,800 acres and provides a scenic backdrop for Trail Ridge Road.

Mount Evans Wilderness is located about 40 miles southwest of Denver. The Mt. Evans Highway forms a non-wilderness corridor into the center of this 70,000 acre wilderness. Elevations range from 8,400 feet to 14,264 foot Mount Evans. Vegetation at higher elevations consists of alpine treeless plains. Significant stands of spruce-fir and lodgepole pine lie below timberline. The wilderness contains the 5,880 acre Abyss Lake Scenic Area, a glacier-carved basin with outstanding scenery.

Indian Peaks Wilderness is located primarily within the Arapaho and Roosevelt national forests, although the northernmost portion is located in Rocky Mountain National Park. The name Indian Peaks was selected because many of the peaks within the wilderness are named for Indian tribes in the West. This 73,391-acre wilderness contains vast areas of alpine tundra, numerous cirque basins with remnant glaciers, and nearly 50 lakes in the shadows of the Continental Divide. Elevations range from 8,400 to 13,000 feet. This is the most frequently visited wilderness in Colorado.

Location

The Arapaho National Forest includes land on both sides of the Continental Divide, which separates the Platte River watersheds that flow to the Atlantic Ocean and the Colorado River watersheds that flow to the Pacific Ocean. Established July 1, 1908 by President Theodore Roosevelt, the 1,025,077-acre forest is named after the plains Indian tribe that frequented the region for summer hunting. The area includes the summit drive to Mount Evans, the highest paved highway in the United States along with 4 wilderness areas.

For Information

Arapaho and Roosevelt National Forest
 Headquarters
240 West Prospect Road
Fort Collins, CO 80526
(303) 498-1100

Clear Creek Ranger District

Campground Locations

Mizpah—7½ miles west of Empire on US 40, from I-70 Exit 233.

Clear Lake and *Guanella Pass*—both on Forest Road 118, south of I-70 at Georgetown: Clear Lake is 5 miles and Guanella Pass is 8 miles.

Echo Lake and *West Chicago Creek*—both on SH 103, southwest from I-70 at Idaho Springs: Echo Lake is 14 miles; and West Chicago Creek Group Campground is 7 miles on SH 103, then 3 miles southwest on Forest Road 188.

Columbine—on SH 279, 2 miles northwest of Central City (due west of SH 119 at Blackhawk).

Pickle Gulch Group Campground—4 miles north of Blackhawk on SH 119; then 2 miles north on a Forest Road.

Cold Springs—on SH 119, 5 miles north of Blackhawk.

This wilderness cabin serves as a rest stop for cross-country skiers.

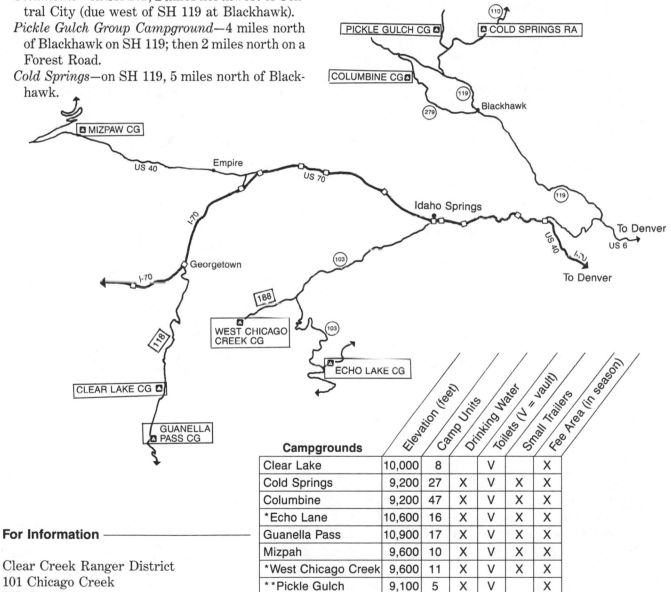

Campgrounds	Elevation (feet)	Camp Units	Drinking Water	Toilets (V = vault)	Small Trailers	Fee Area (in season)
Clear Lake	10,000	8		V		X
Cold Springs	9,200	27	X	V	X	X
Columbine	9,200	47	X	V	X	X
*Echo Lane	10,600	16	X	V	X	X
Guanella Pass	10,900	17	X	V	X	X
Mizpah	9,600	10	X	V	X	X
*West Chicago Creek	9,600	11	X	V	X	X
**Pickle Gulch	9,100	5	X	V		X

   * On MISTIX reservation system.

  ** Group campgrounds (30 people/site); reservations required.

For Information

Clear Creek Ranger District
101 Chicago Creek
P.O. Box 3307
Idaho Springs, CO 80452
(303) 567-2901

Sulphur Ranger District

Campground Locations

Three campgrounds, all on Lake Granby and in the Arapaho National Recreation Area are located north of Granby off of US 34:

—*Arapaho Bay* is on the east end of Lake Granby; travel 6½ miles north from Granby, then 9 miles east on County Road 6. There are 3 campground loops: Big Rock, Moraine & Roaring Fork.

—*Stillwater* is on the northwest shore of Lake Granby, just 6½ miles south of Grand Lake.

—*Cutthroat Bay Group Campground*, is just a few miles north of the Stillwater Campground.

Green Ridge—also in the Arapaho NRA is on the south end of Shadow Mountain Lake; 3 miles southwest of Grand Lake on US 34, then 1 mile southeast on County Road 66.

Willow Creek—also in the Arapaho NRA, is on Willow Creek Reservoir; from Granby, travel 6½ miles northeast on US 34, then 3½ miles west on County Road 40.

Denver Creek and *Sawmill Gulch*—both located along SH 125 northwest of Granby via US 40. Sawmill is approximately 13 miles and Denver Creek is an additional 2 miles.

Tabernash—along US 40 about midway between Granby and Tabernash.

For Information

Sulphur Ranger District
62429 US Highway 40
P.O. Box 10
Granby, CO 80446
(303) 887-3331

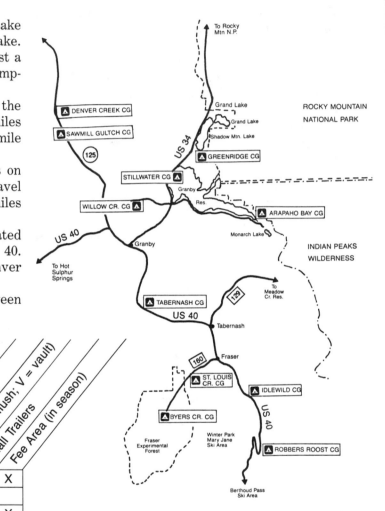

Campgrounds	Elevation (feet)	Camp Units	Drinking Water	Toilets (F = flush; V = vault)	Small Trailers	Fee Area (in season)
Arapaho Bay	8,320	84	X	V	X	X
Byers Creek	9,360	6	X	V	X	
Denver Creek	8,800	22	X	V		X
*Green Ridge	8,360	77	X	F	X	X
Idlewild	9,000	24	X	V	X	X
Robbers Roost	9,826	11	X	V	X	X
Sawmill Gulch	8,700	5	X	V		X
St. Louis Creek	8,900	18	X	V	X	X
*Stillwater	8,300	148	X	F	X	X
Tabernash	8,600	36		V	X	
Willow Creek	8,130	34	X	V		X
**Cutthroat Bay	8,500			V	X	X

* On MISTIX reservation system.
** Group campground; reservation required.

Byers Creek and *St. Louis Creek*—both located in the Fraser Experimental Forest southwest of US 40 at Fraser. Take Forest Road 160 southwest from Fraser; St. Louis Creek is 3 miles and Byers Creek is 6½ miles.

Idlewild and *Robbers Roost*—both located south of Fraser on US 40; Idlewild is 4 miles from town and Robbers Roost is 9½ miles.

Arapaho National Recreation Area

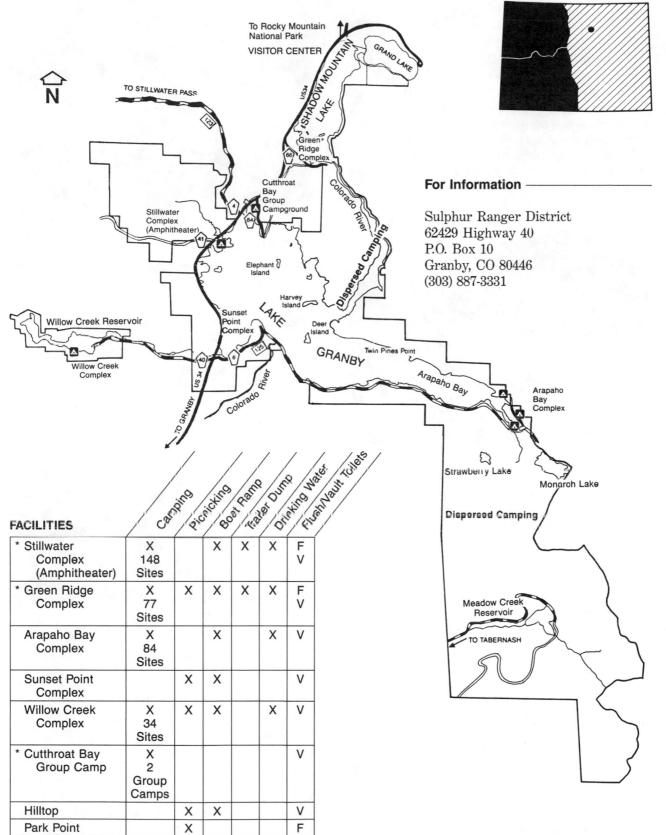

To Rocky Mountain National Park

VISITOR CENTER

TO STILLWATER PASS

N

TO STILLWATER PASS

123

SHADOW MOUNTAIN LAKE

GRAND LAKE

US 34

Green Ridge Complex

66

Cutthroat Bay Group Campground

4

64

Stillwater Complex (Amphitheater)

41

Colorado River

Elephant Island

Harvey Island

Deer Island

LAKE

Dispersed Camping

Sunset Point Complex

Willow Creek Reservoir

Willow Creek Complex

40

6

125

US 34

TO GRANBY

Colorado River

GRANBY

Twin Pines Point

Arapaho Bay

Arapaho Bay Complex

Strawberry Lake

Monarch Lake

Dispersed Camping

Meadow Creek Reservoir

TO TABERNASH

For Information

Sulphur Ranger District
62429 Highway 40
P.O. Box 10
Granby, CO 80446
(303) 887-3331

FACILITIES	Camping	Picnicking	Boat Ramp	Trailer Dump	Drinking Water	Flush/Vault Toilets
* Stillwater Complex (Amphitheater)	X 148 Sites		X	X	X	F V
* Green Ridge Complex	X 77 Sites	X	X	X	X	F V
Arapaho Bay Complex	X 84 Sites		X		X	V
Sunset Point Complex		X	X			V
Willow Creek Complex	X 34 Sites	X	X		X	V
* Cutthroat Bay Group Camp	X 2 Group Camps					V
Hilltop		X	X			V
Park Point		X				F

* On MISTIX reservation system.

Arapaho National Recreation Area *(continued)*

Location

The Arapaho National Recreation Area is adjacent to Rocky Mountain National Park to the northeast and is accessible from the north via Trail Ridge Road (US 34) and from the west and south via US 40 at Granby. The 36,000-acre Arapaho National Recreation Area was established by Congress in 1978; it is administered by the Sulphur Ranger District of the Arapaho National Forest. Elevations range from 8,200 to 11,000 feet.

The campsites at Sillwater Campground are quite spacious.

About the Recreation Area

The Arapaho National Recreation Area is a scenic water wonderland in the upper reaches of the Colorado River Valley. It contains five major lakes: Lake Granby, Shadow Mountain Reservoir, Monarch Lake, Willow Creek Reservoir, and Meadow Creek Reservoir. Together, with the adjacent Grand Lake, the lakes and reservoirs are often referred to as the "Great Lakes of Colorado." Water levels may change as several of the lakes are part of the Colorado-Big Thompson Water Diversion Project, and water needs must also be met on the eastern slope.

Recreation at Lake Granby (7,256 acres) includes power and sailboating, water skiing, wind surfing, and fishing. It is the second largest body of water in Colorado. The 1,400-acre Shadow Mountain Reservoir is maintained at a constant level equal to the elevation of Grand Lake and is connected by a canal allowing boat passage between the two. Monarch

Lake Granby is the second largest body of water in Colorado.

Lake (150 acres) is a constant level lake, open to nonmotorized watercraft only. The 50-acre Meadow Creek Reservoir, located in the most remote part of the recreation area at nearly 10,000 feet in elevation, is also open to nonmotorized watercraft only. Power boats are allowed at the 750-acre Willow Creek reservoir, but are restricted to a "no wake" speed.

These tent campers have a beautiful view of Lake Granby.

The waters of the Arapaho National Recreation Area are open year-round to fishing, subject to Colorado regulations. Ice fishing is very popular from late December through the end of February. The Stillwater Boat Launch parking area is plowed in the winter and provides parking for snowmobilers and ice anglers. Although no marked snowmobile or cross-country ski trails are set up in the Arapaho National Recreation Area, both activities are allowed.

Barbour Ponds State Recreation Area

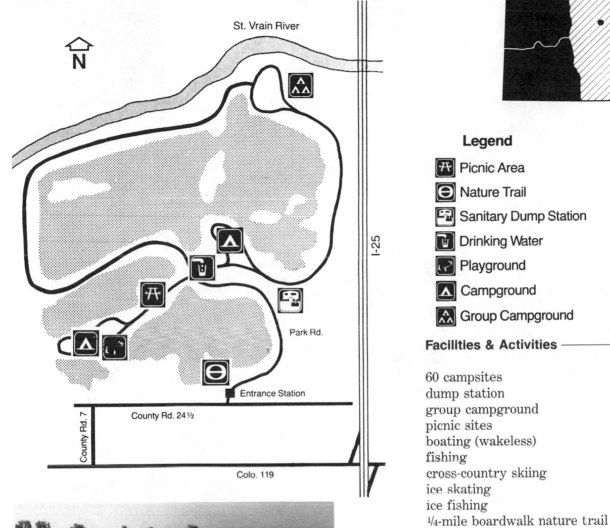

St. Vrain River

N

I-25

Park Rd.

Entrance Station

County Rd. 7

County Rd. 24½

Colo. 119

Legend

- 🏕 Picnic Area
- ⊖ Nature Trail
- 🚰 Sanitary Dump Station
- 🚰 Drinking Water
- 🛝 Playground
- ⛺ Campground
- ⛺ Group Campground

Facilities & Activities

60 campsites
dump station
group campground
picnic sites
boating (wakeless)
fishing
cross-country skiing
ice skating
ice fishing
¼-mile boardwalk nature trail

Location

Barbour Ponds State Recreation Area is located 7 miles east of US 287 at Longmont and west of I-25 off of SH 119; turn north on County Road 7. Although small, with only 50 land acres and 80 water acres, the setting is scenic and convenient. The park's four quiet ponds offer some of the best warm-water fishing in northern Colorado. Elevation: 4,900 feet.

For Information

Barbour Ponds State Recreation Area
c/o Boyd Lake State Recreation Area
3720 N. County Rd., Box 11-C
Loveland, CO 80538
(303) 669-1739

This plant along the nature trail at Barbour Ponds is the center of attention for this photographer.

Bear Creek Lake Park

For Information

City of Lakewood
Parks and Recreation Department
455 South Allison Parkway
Lakewood, CO 80226
(303) 987-7800

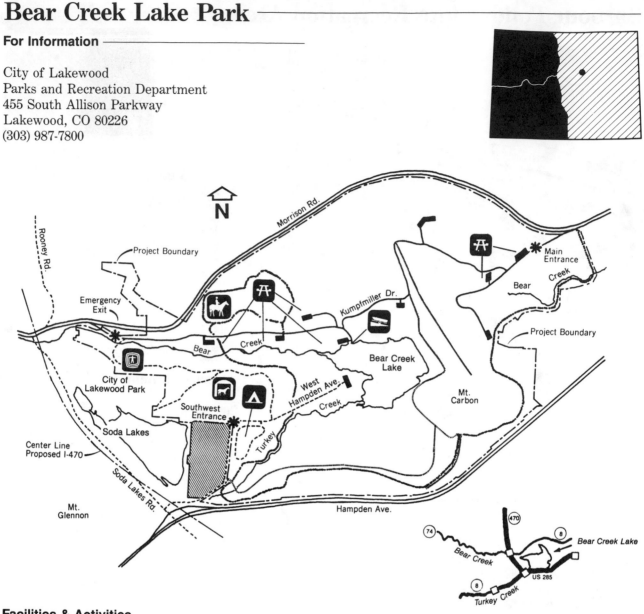

Facilities & Activities

camping (Soda Lakes only)
picnicking
group picnic pavilions
Marina (Soda Lakes)
   rentals: paddles boats, rowboats, canoes, sail-
   boats, sailboards
   lessons: sailboarding, canoeing, sailboating
boating
   motorless at Soda Lakes
   wakeless at Bear Creek Lake (less than 5 h.p.)
boat ramps
fishing
ice fishing
nature trail
horseback trails

Location

Bear Creek Lake Park is located ½ mile west of
Kipling Street on Morrison Road in Lakewood (10
miles southwest of downtown Denver). The dam
was constructed by the U.S. Army Corps of Engi-
neers primarily for flood control of Bear Creek and
Turkey Creek. The land was leased to the city of
Lakewood in 1982 to be developed as a recreational
area. Elevations in the 2,448-acre park range from
5,500 feet to 5,775 feet at the top of Mount Carbon.
Soda Lakes is an extension of Bear Creek Lake
Park and is owned and operated by the city of Lake-
wood. A total of 275 acres encompasses this area.
Soda Lakes is located east of Soda Lakes Road on
Old Hampden Frontage Road.

Bonny State Recreation Area

Facilities & Activities

201 campsites
showers
dump station
laundry
picnic sites
group picnic area available
swimming
snackbar
boating
boat ramps

marina
boat rental
fishing
fish cleaning station
water skiing
sailboarding
cross-country skiing
ice skating
ice fishing
winter camping

For Information

Bonny State Recreation Area
3010 County Rd. 3, Box 78-A
Idalia, CO 80735
(303) 354-7306

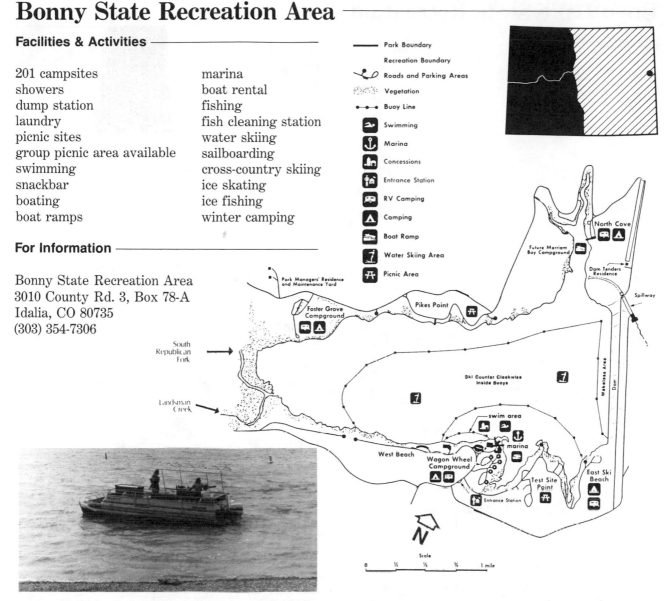

| Park Boundary |
| Recreation Boundary |
| Roads and Parking Areas |
| Vegetation |
| Buoy Line |
| Swimming |
| Marina |
| Concessions |
| Entrance Station |
| RV Camping |
| Camping |
| Boat Ramp |
| Water Skiing Area |
| Picnic Area |

Deck boats are extremely popular on the Colorado lakes.

Campground	Flush toilets	Vault toilets	Showers	Laundry	Boat ramp	Water
Foster Grove	•	•				•
North Cove		•			•	
East Beach		•				•
Wagon Wheel	•	•	•	•	X	•

• Facility in campground
x Facility within walking distance

Location

Bonny State Recreation Area is located 23 miles north of I-70 at Burlington and south of US 36 off of US 385. Travel east on County Road 2 or 3 to reach the 1,900 surface acre reservoir. Located in the broad valley of the South Fork of the Republican River, the park, although well known as a spring and summer water sports area, offers a variety of year-round recreational opportunities. Willow trees and large cottonwoods are characteristic of the 3,700-foot elevation. Bonny SRA has 5,000 land acres and is jointly administered: the Colorado Division of Parks and Outdoor Recreation manages the recreational facilities and services, and the Colorado Division of Wildlife has jurisdiction over the fish and wildlife resources.

Boyd Lake State Recreation Area

For Information

Boyd Lake State Recreation Area
3720 N. County Rd., Box 11-C
Loveland, CO 80538
(303) 669-1739

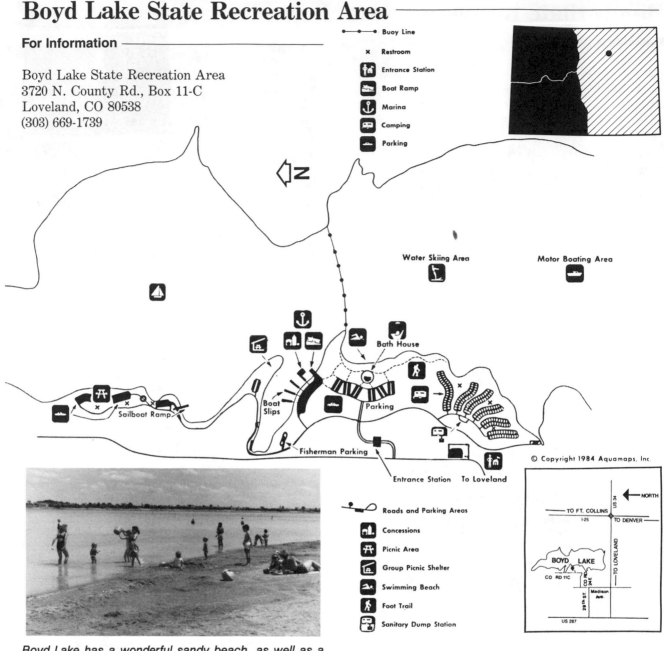

Buoy Line
× Restroom
Entrance Station
Boat Ramp
Marina
Camping
Parking

Water Skiing Area
Motor Boating Area

Bath House

Boat Slips
Parking

Sailboat Ramp

Fisherman Parking

Entrance Station   To Loveland

© Copyright 1984 Aquamaps, Inc.

Roads and Parking Areas
Concessions
Picnic Area
Group Picnic Shelter
Swimming Beach
Foot Trail
Sanitary Dump Station

TO FT. COLLINS   NORTH
I-25   TO DENVER
BOYD   LAKE
CO RD 11C
29th ST   Madison Ave
US 287   TO LOVELAND

Boyd Lake has a wonderful sandy beach, as well as a bathhouse.

Facilities & Activities

148 campsites	marina
showers	boat rental
dump station	fishing
picnic sites	fish cleaning station
group picnic area available	water skiing
swimming	sailboarding
bathhouse	sailboard rental
snackbar	cross-country skiing
boating	ice skating
boat ramps	ice fishing

Location

Boyd Lake State Recreation Area is located 1 mile northeast of Loveland; from US 34 travel north on Madison Avenue and follow the signs or from US 287 travel east on 29th Street and follow the signs on County Roads 24E and 11C. With 1,747 surface-acres when full, Boyd Lake SRA is rapidly becoming a water sports haven for northern Colorado. The entire two-mile-long lake is open to boating and sailing, but only the south end of the lake is open for water skiing. Boyd Lake is the site of a variety of regattas and annual hydroplane races. Elevation: 5,000 feet.

Chatfield State Recreation Area

For Information

Chatfield State Recreation Area
11500 N. Roxborough Park Rd.
Littleton, CO 80125
(303) 791-7275

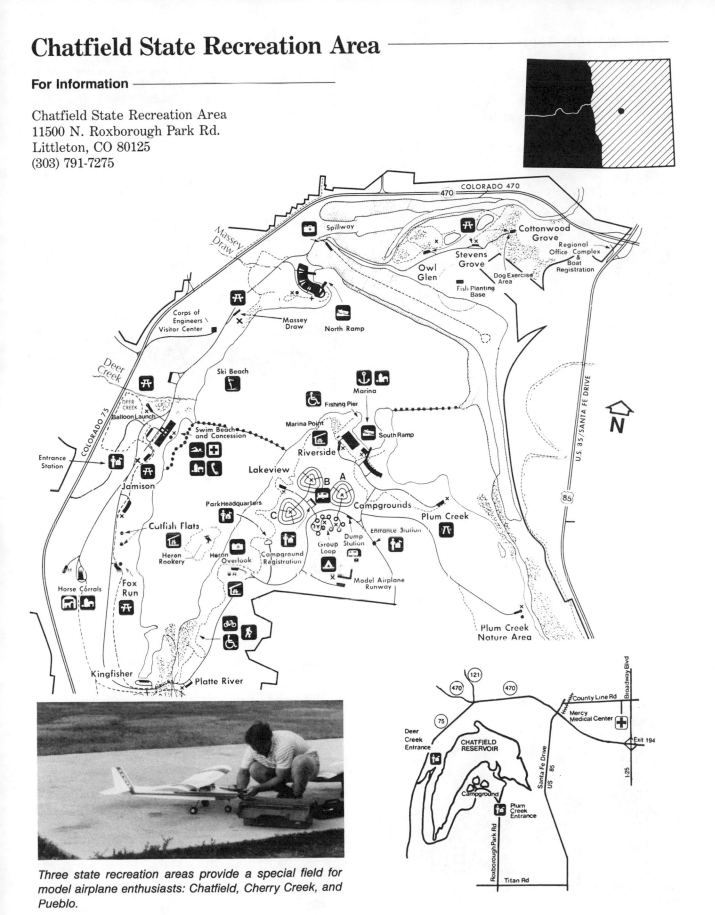

Three state recreation areas provide a special field for model airplane enthusiasts: Chatfield, Cherry Creek, and Pueblo.

REGION 2

Chatfield State Recreation Area *(continued)*

Two ramps provide boat access to the 1,450-surface-acre Chatfield Lake.

Location

Chatfield State Recreation Area is one of Colorado's most complete outdoor recreation areas. South of Denver, the park is located west of US 85, east of SH 75 and south of SH 470. When traveling from I-25, take exit 194 to reach SH 470. From SH 470, the Deer Creek Entrance is off of SH 75 and the Plum Creek Entrance is off of US 85 via west on Titan Road, then north on Roxborough Park Road (see vicinity map). Chatfield Dam, completed in 1976 by the U.S. Army Corps of Engineers as a flood control measure on the South Platte River and Plum Creek, impounds 1,450 surface acres of water. The 5,600-acre park is administered by the Colorado Division of Parks and Outdoor Recreation. A 27-acre heron rookery is the breeding area

The Great Blue Heron can be viewed from the observation area overlooking the 27-acre rookery.

for over 50 pairs of the large birds. Paved runways are provided for radio-controlled model airplanes. A launch site for hot air balloons is located near the Deer Creek entrance. Elevation: 5,500 feet.

The sailboat marina is located near the south boat ramp.

Facilities & Activities

153 campsites
  51 with electrical hookups
showers
dump station
laundry
group campground
picnic sites
group picnic area available
swimming
bathhouse
snackbar
boating (½ is wakeless)
boat ramps
marina
boat rental
fishing
water skiing
sailboarding
sailboard rental
model airplane field
hot air balloon launching pad
cross-country skiing
ice skating
ice fishing
snow tubing
18 miles of hiking trails
18 miles of bicycling trails
24 miles of horseback trails
stables/horse rental

Cherry Creek State Recreation Area

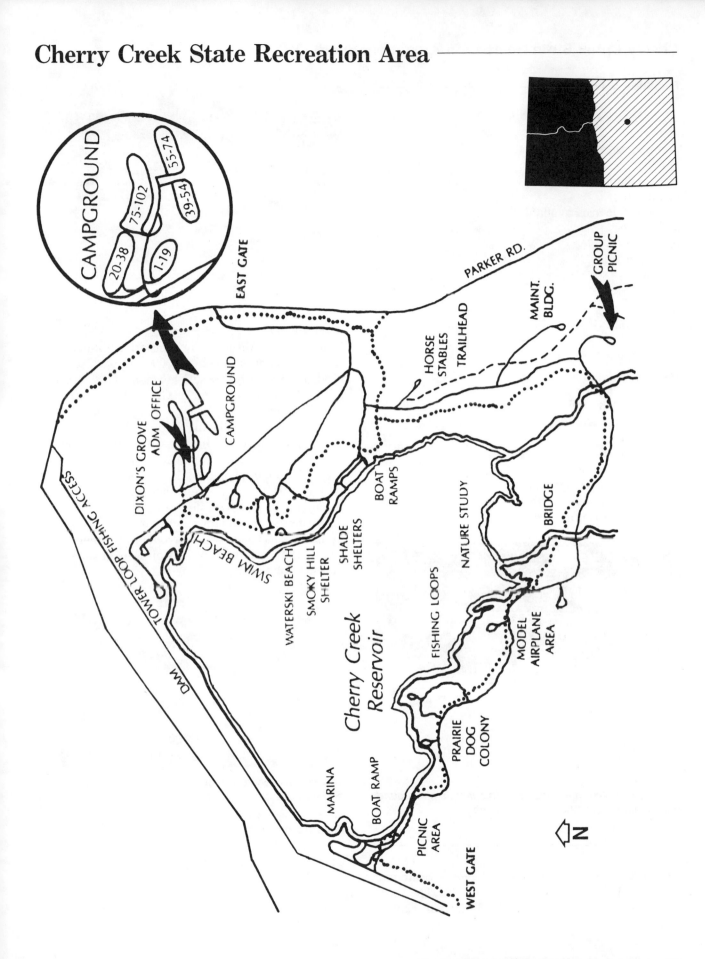

CAMPGROUND

55-74
39-54
75-102
20-38
1-19

EAST GATE

PARKER RD.

GROUP PICNIC

HORSE STABLES
TRAILHEAD
MAINT. BLDG.

CAMPGROUND

DIXON'S GROVE
ADM. OFFICE

TOWER LOOP FISHING ACCESS

DAM

SWIM BEACH

WATERSKI BEACH
SMOKY HILL SHELTER
SHADE SHELTERS
BOAT RAMPS

NATURE STUDY
BRIDGE

FISHING LOOPS

Cherry Creek Reservoir

MODEL AIRPLANE AREA

PRAIRIE DOG COLONY

MARINA
BOAT RAMP

PICNIC AREA

WEST GATE

N

REGION.2

Cherry Creek State Recreation Area *(continued)*

Facilities & Activities

102 campsites
showers
dump station
laundry
group campground
picnic sites
group picnic area available
swimming
bathhouse
snackbar
boating
boat ramps
marina
boat rental
fishing
water skiing
sailboarding
sailboard rental
model airplane field
cross-country skiing
ice skating
ice fishing
12 miles of hiking trails
11 miles of bicycling trails
12 miles of horseback trails
stables/horse rental

Cherry Creek has lifeguards on duty during peak periods.

from I-225 in Aurora. The recreational opportunities are unlimited at this 3,900-acre park, considered an oasis for boaters, fishermen, and swimmers alike. The 880-acre Cherry Creek Reservoir was completed in 1950 by the U.S. Army Corps of Engineers to prevent flooding. The recreational facilities are administered by the Colorado Division of Parks and Outdoor Recreation. Each year more than 1.5 million people come to Cherry Creek. To protect park users, prevent damage to the natural resources, and provide for a more enjoyable stay for visitors, a maximum number of visitors allowed in the park has been set. To avoid inconvenience, arrive at the park early or visit on weekdays or evenings. Elevation: 5,500 feet.

A few youngsters are enticed by this unique playground equipment on the Cherry Creek beach.

There's definitely a "people-watcher" in this group . . . and his eyes are on the swimming beach!

Location

Cherry Creek State Recreation Area is located in southeast Denver 1.5 miles south of I-225. The East Gate entrance is on Parker Road (SH 83), Exit 4

For Information

Cherry Creek State Recreation Area
4201 S. Parker Rd.
Aurora, CO 80014
(303) 699-3860

Eleven-Mile State Recreation Area

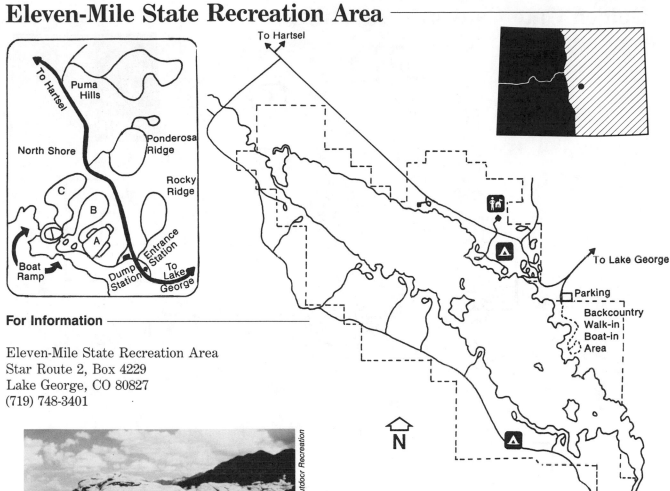

For Information

Eleven-Mile State Recreation Area
Star Route 2, Box 4229
Lake George, CO 80827
(719) 748-3401

Yep! Northern pike really are in Eleven-Mile Reservoir!

Colorado Division of Parks and Outdoor Recreation

Location

Eleven-Mile State Recreation Area is located west of Colorado Springs. Travel on US 24 for 38 miles to Lake George; one mile west of Lake George turn left on County Rd. 92 and follow the pavement for 10 miles. The Pike National Forest borders the park on two sides. In the distance, Pike's Peak to the east and the snowy Continental Divide to the west form an imposing setting for the 3,405-acre reservoir, one of the state's best trout and northern pike fisheries. The reservoir and 4,075 land acres, managed by the Colorado Division

of Parks and Outdoor Recreation, are under a lease from the Denver Water Board. Eleven-Mile SRA's 8,566-foot altitude means that temperatures can vary widely in any season.

Facilities & Activities

240 campsites
dump station
25 backcountry campsites available
picnic sites
boating (special restrictions)
boat ramps
fishing
sailboarding
cross-country skiing
ice skating
ice fishing
snow tubing
winter camping
1½ miles of hiking trails
horseback riding

Golden Gate Canyon State Park

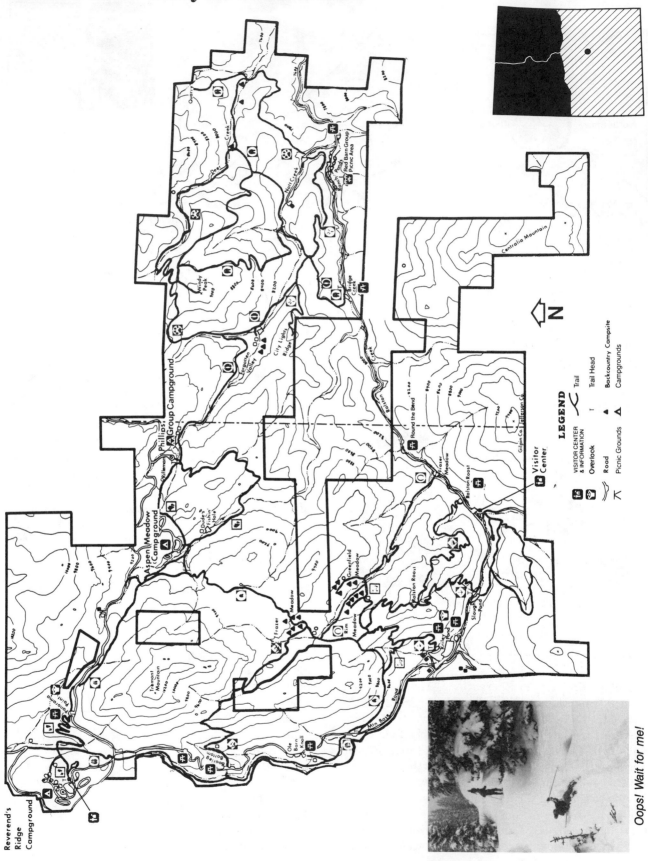

LEGEND

VISITOR CENTER & INFORMATION

Overlook

Road

Picnic Grounds

Trail

Trail Head

Backcountry Campsite

Campgrounds

Visitor Center

Oops! Wait for me!

Reverend's Ridge Campground

Golden Gate Canyon State Park *(continued)*

Aspen Meadow campground at Golden Gate Canyon is a "tents-only" campground.

Location

Golden Gate Canyon State Park, with 10,200 acres of beauty ranging in elevation from 7,600 to 10,400 feet, is within an hour's drive west of the Denver area via I-70. The park may be reached by traveling north from Idaho Springs toward Nederland on SH 119; turn right and follow signs to the park. Or, take SH 93 north from Golden for 1.5 miles to the Golden Gate Canyon Road. Turn left and continue for 15 miles to the visitor's center. The 7,000 backcountry acres offer opportunities for primitive camping as well as 13 trails, each marked with an animal footprint, with the difficulty indicated by the background shape and color of the marker.

Large motor homes welcome the pull-through sites available at some campgrounds.

Facilities & Activities

164 campsites
showers
dump station
laundry
group campground
24 backcountry campsites available
visitor/nature center
picnic sites
group picnic area available
fishing
rock climbing
cross-country skiing
ice skating
ice fishing
snow tubing
winter camping
48 miles of hiking trails
26 miles of horseback trails

Winter is a beautiful time of the year to visit the parks—a variety of winter activities is available.

For Information

Golden Gate Canyon State Park
Route 6, Box 280
Golden, Co 80403
(303) 592-1502

Jackson Lake State Recreation Area

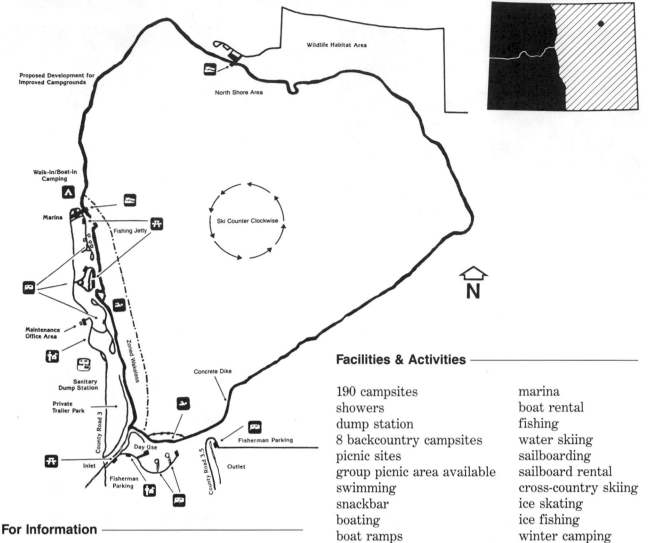

Facilities & Activities

190 campsites	marina
showers	boat rental
dump station	fishing
8 backcountry campsites	water skiing
picnic sites	sailboarding
group picnic area available	sailboard rental
swimming	cross-country skiing
snackbar	ice skating
boating	ice fishing
boat ramps	winter camping

For Information

Jackson Lake State Recreation Area
26363 County Rd. 3
Orchard, CO 80649
(303) 645-2551

Location

Jackson Lake State Recreation Area is located east of Fort Collins and 80 miles northeast of Denver. From Exit 66 at the I-76/US 34 Interchange, take SH 39 north 7¼ miles through Goodrich. Continue straight ahead on SH 144 to a "T" intersection approximately ½ mile north of Goodrich; turn left; proceed west, then north, on a paved road for 2½ miles to the park boundary. The park has a land area of 440 acres and a 2,700 surface-area lake. The recreation area is famed for its shoreline camping and the large, warm-water reservoir with its sandy bottom and beaches. Elevation: 4,400 feet.

Jackson Lake is famed for its shoreline camping.

Lake Hasty Recreation Area/John Martin Reservoir

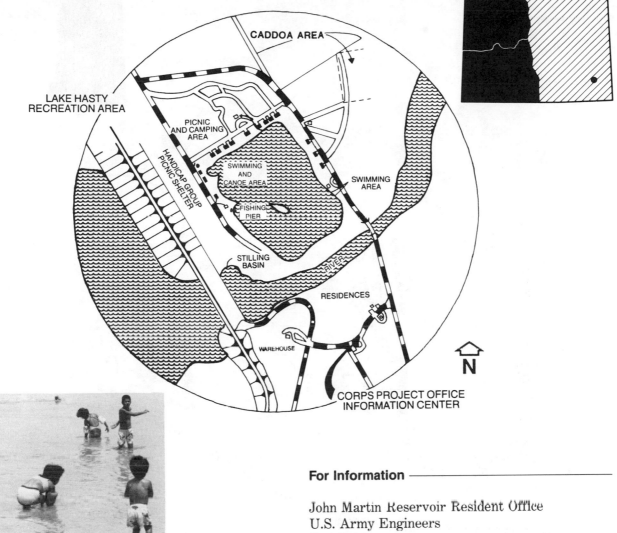

Happiness is a day at the beach!

Location

Lake Hasty Recreation Area is located downstream from the dam and the north shore of John Martin Reservoir. The reservoir, completed in 1948, is located on the Arkansas River, south of US 50 between LaJunta and Lamar. In Hasty, turn south and travel approximately 3 miles to Lake Hasty Recreation Area and John Martin Reservoir. The reservoir, part of the comprehensive plan for flood control, is operated by the Albuquerque District of the U.S. Army Corps of Engineers. The recreation area, a center of year-round recreation, was formed from a 75-acre tract excavated for earthfill for the dam and filled with water.

For Information

John Martin Reservoir Resident Office
U.S. Army Engineers
Star Route
Hasty, CO 81044
(719) 336-3476

Facilities & Activities at Lake Hasty Recreation Area

51 campsites	playgrounds
dispersed camping	swimming area
trailer dump station	motorless boating
picnic shelters	fishing
amphitheater	fishing pier

Facilities & Activities at John Martin Reservoir

information center (slide show)	boating
boat ramp at Overlook	water skiing
picnicking at Overlook	fishing
swimming	

Lathrop State Park

For Information

Lathrop State Park
70 County Rd. 502
Walsenburg, CO 81089
(719) 738-2376

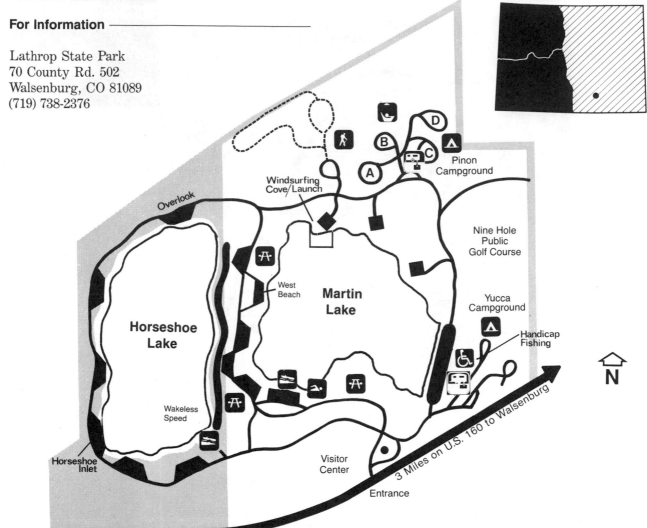

ology, culture, and legends. Stop at the visitor center to see the murals depicting local history. The park has 1,050 land acres and 320 water acres in Horseshoe Lake and Martin Lake. Migrating ducks stop at the lakes to rest. Elevation: 6,400 feet.

Lathrop has a designated swimming area at Martin Lake but does not provide lifeguards.

Location

Lathrop State Park is located 3 miles west of Walsenburg on the north side of US 160. The Spanish Peaks (13,610 feet and 12,669 feet) rise in the distance like sentinels over an area rich in history, ge-

Facilities & Activities

98 campsites	fishing
electrical hookups	water skiing
showers	sailboarding
dump station	9-hole golf course
laundry	cross-country skiing
group campground	ice skating
visitor/nature center	ice fishing
picnic sites	snow tubing
swimming	winter camping
bathhouse	2 miles of hiking trails
boating	4 miles of bicycling trails
boat ramps	horseback riding

Lory State Park

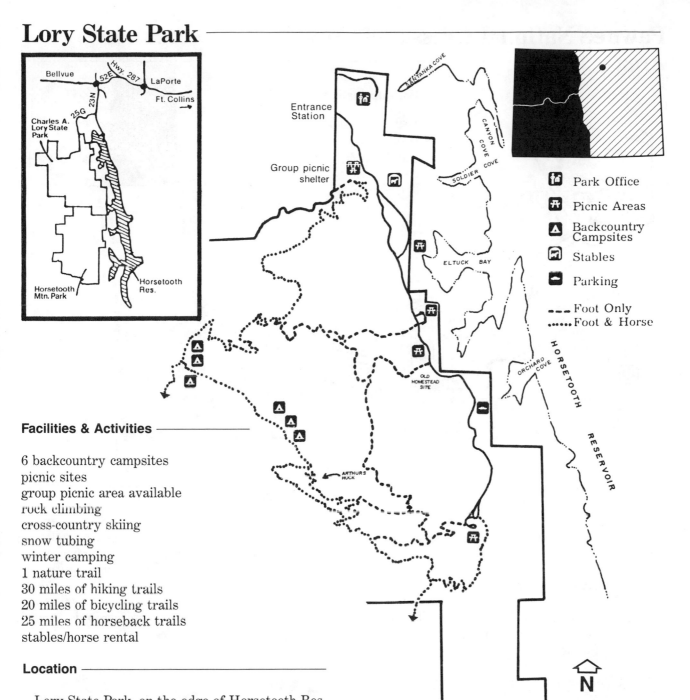

Park Office

Picnic Areas

Backcountry Campsites

Stables

Parking

--- Foot Only
..... Foot & Horse

Facilities & Activities

6 backcountry campsites
picnic sites
group picnic area available
rock climbing
cross-country skiing
snow tubing
winter camping
1 nature trail
30 miles of hiking trails
20 miles of bicycling trails
25 miles of horseback trails
stables/horse rental

Location

Lory State Park, on the edge of Horsetooth Reservoir, is west of Fort Collins. From Fort Collins take US 287 north through La Porte. At the Bellvue exit (County Rd. 52E) turn left, drive 1 mile to County Rd. 23N. Turn left and go 1.4 miles to County Rd. 25G. Turn right and go 1.6 miles to the park entrance. This four-season park is noted for its rock formations and for terrain and vegetation that change with the altitude. Park boundaries preserve 2,479 acres of the transition ecology of the Rocky Mountain foothills. With 2,000 backcountry acres, Lory is one of the premier equestrian centers in the state park system and is a great park for hikers.

The park offers overnight backcountry camping at 6 designated sites; no motorized or vehicular overnight camping is permitted.

For Information

Lory State Park
708 Lodgepole Drive
Bellvue, CO 80512
(303) 493-1623

Pawnee National Grassland/Crow Valley Recreation Area

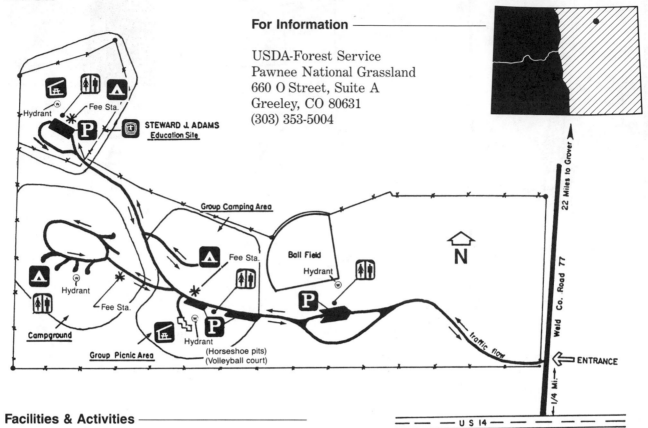

For Information

USDA-Forest Service
Pawnee National Grassland
660 O Street, Suite A
Greeley, CO 80631
(303) 353-5004

Facilities & Activities

5 campsites
  each with parking spur, table, fire ring and barbeque grill
group camping area
group picnic area (reservations allow users exclusive use)
  32 picnic tables plus a shelter house with a covered barbecue and serving area, electricity and lights; volleyball court and horseshoe pit.
education site (reservation required)
  shelter house with lights and electricity, 5 picnic tables, group fire circle
ball field
water & toilet facilities for each area

Location

Pawnee National Grassland is located northeast of Fort Collins; north of SH 14 and east of US 85. Pawnee's one developed recreation facility—Crow Valley Recreation Area—is reached by traveling one-fourth mile north on County Road 77 from SH 14 at Briggsdale, then left to the recreation area. Crow Valley Recreation Area consists of five separate and individual facilities providing a variety of recreational opportunities to the general public: ball field, group picnic area, group camping area, family campground, and an area for educational groups. The education site accommodates both day use and overnight camping for those wishing to study, observe, or enjoy the shortgrass prairie environment. Elevation: 4,900 feet.

Enjoy this mushroom for its unique beauty, but don't be tempted to eat it.

Pike National Forest

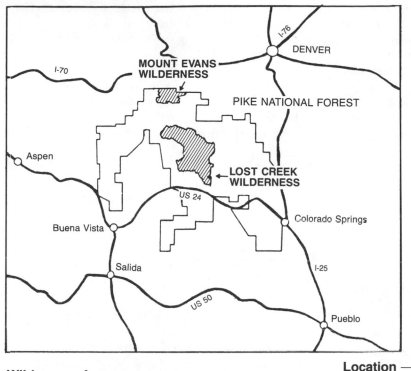

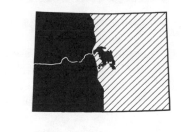

For Information

Pike and San Isabel National Forest
   Headquarters
1920 Valley Drive
Pueblo, CO 81008
(719) 545-8737

Wilderness Areas

Mount Evans Wilderness is located about 40 miles southwest of Denver. The Mt. Evans Highway forms a non-wilderness corridor into the center of this 73,000-acre wilderness. Elevations range from 8,400 feet to 14,264 foot Mount Evans. Another "fourteener," Mt. Bierstadt, is within the wilderness in the 5,880-acre Abyss Lake Scenic Area, a glacier-carved basin with outstanding scenery. Vegetation at higher elevations consists of alpine treeless plains. Significant stands of spruce-fir and lodgepole pine lie below timberline.

Lost Creek Wilderness is less than 40 miles southwest of Denver, and has a wide variety of terrain and vegetation types. This 106,000-acre wilderness ranges from steep rock slopes up to 12,431 at Bison Peak to high mountain meadows and deep canyons to a low of about 8,000 feet elevation. Lost creek, with its unique and outstanding scenic quality, contains bold outcrops of Pikes Peak granite that have been carved into an infinite variety of forms and shapes by the forces of erosion. Great dome-like forms, spires, turrets and ridges characterize the landscape. Talus slopes of huge boulders are common. Stream courses are tortuous and have in places carved underground channels through the talus debris.

Location

Pike National Forest lies west of I-25 between Denver and Colorado Springs. This 1,106,604-acre forest contains many of Colorado's "fourteeners"—mountain peaks over 14,000 feet in elevation. Pikes Peak, at 14,110 feet, is the forest's most famous landmark. It was named for Lt. Zebulon Pike who sighted the peak from the distant plains in November 1806. He and his men were unable to climb the peak, but today thousands of people reach the summit each year by the auto road, a cog railway, and a hiking trail.

Special Notes

Winding mountain roads such as the Pikes Peak Highway, the Gold Camp Road, and the Rampart Range Road, provide interesting auto touring around Colorado Springs. Areas such as the Windy-Ridge Bristlecone Pine Scenic Area provide excellent scenery for the hiker and backpacker. Located 4 miles northwest of Alma, it was established in July 1967 to protect a unique grove of beautifully grotesque and deformed bristlecone pine trees. Thousands of people reach the top of Pikes Peak each year on the toll road; thousands of others reach the top via the "cog road"; but thousands more hike up the Barr Trail from Manitou Springs. This 11.7-mile trail was designated a National Recreation Trail in 1979.

REGION 2

Pikes Peak Ranger District

Campground Locations

Meadow Ridge and *Thunder Ridge* campgrounds are both located at the Rampart Reservoir Recreation Area east of Woodland Park on the Rampart Range Road. From Woodland Park go 4½ miles northeast on Forest Road 393, then 4 miles southeast on Forest Road 300 (Rampart Range Road). Then 1½ miles northeast on Forest Road 306.

The Manitou Park Area north of Woodland Park along SH 67 has 3 campgrounds:
- —*South Meadows* is 5¾ miles north of Woodland Park;
- —*Colorado* is 7 miles north; and
- —*Painted Rocks* is 8 miles north, then ½ mile west on Forest Road 341.

Wildhorn—8 miles north of Florissant off of Forest Road 200; turn left on Forest Road 361 and go ¾ mile.

Trail Creek—approximately 5 miles beyond Wildhorn Campground on Forest Road 200 and 3 miles south of the town of Westcreek.

Big Turkey—southwest of Westcreek; go 1 mile south, then 4 miles southwest on Forest Road 360.

The Crags—off of US 24 at Divide; go south on SH 67 for 4½ miles; then east on Forest Road 383 for 3½ miles.

Single file, Indian style!

Campgrounds	Elevation (feet)	Camp Units	Drinking Water	Toilets (V = vault)	Small Trailers	Fee Area (in season)
Big Turkey	7,800	10	X	V	X	
Colorado	7,800	63	X	V	X	X
*Meadow Ridge	9,200	19	X	V	X	X
Painted Rocks	7,800	15	X	V	X	X
South Meadows	8,000	57	X	V	X	X
The Crags	10,100	17	X	V	X	
*Thunder Ridge	9,200	21	X	V	X	X
Trail Creek	7,800	7	X	V	X	
Wildhorn	9,100	10	X	V	X	

* On MISTIX reservation system.
Group campgrounds: Pike Community, Redrocks and Springdale.

For Information

Pikes Peak Ranger District
601 South Weber Street
Colorado Springs, CO 80903
(719) 636-1602

South Park Ranger District

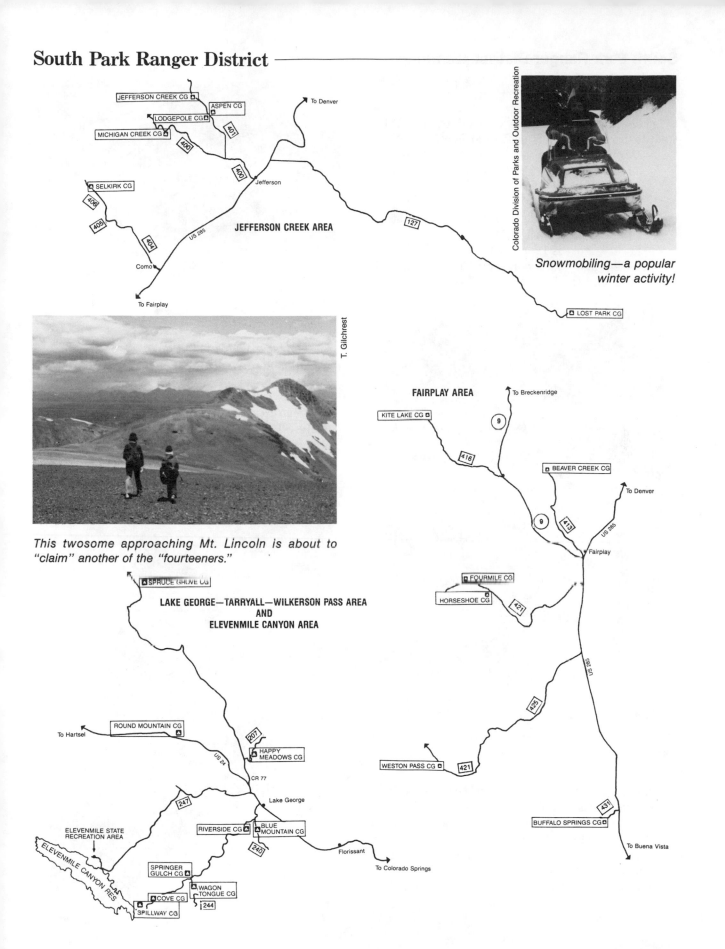

JEFFERSON CREEK CG

ASPEN CG

LODGEPOLE CG

MICHIGAN CREEK CG

401

400

To Denver

SELKIRK CG

406

405

404

400

Jefferson

JEFFERSON CREEK AREA

127

US 285

Como

To Fairplay

LOST PARK CG

Snowmobiling—a popular
winter activity!

This twosome approaching Mt. Lincoln is about to
"claim" another of the "fourteeners."

FAIRPLAY AREA

To Breckenridge

KITE LAKE CG

9

416

BEAVER CREEK CG

To Denver

9

413

US 285

Fairplay

FOURMILE CG

HORSESHOE CG

421

SPRUCE GROVE CG

LAKE GEORGE—TARRYALL—WILKERSON PASS AREA
AND
ELEVENMILE CANYON AREA

ROUND MOUNTAIN CG

To Hartsel

207

US 24

HAPPY
MEADOWS CG

CR 77

247

Lake George

ELEVENMILE STATE
RECREATION AREA

ELEVENMILE CANYON RES

RIVERSIDE CG

BLUE
MOUNTAIN CG

240

Florissant

To Colorado Springs

SPRINGER
GULCH CG

WAGON
TONGUE CG

COVE CG

244

SPILLWAY CG

425

WESTON PASS CG

421

BUFFALO SPRINGS CG

431

To Buena Vista

US 285

South Park Ranger District (continued)

Campground Locations

Three campgrounds are located in the Lake George-Tarryall-Wilkerson Pass area off of US 24:
—*Happy Meadows* is 1¼ miles northwest of Lake George on US 24; then 1¼ miles north on County Road 77; then ¾ mile northeast on Forest Road 207.
—*Round Mountain* is 5½ miles northwest of Lake George on US 24.
—*Spruce Grove* is 1¼ miles northwest on US 24; then 12½ miles north on County Road 77 (beyond the little town of Tarryall).

Have you ever considered skiing to your campsite?

—*Springer Gulch* is 6½ miles.
—*Wagon Tongue* is 7 miles; then left on Forest Road 244 for ½ mile.
—*Cove* is 9.3 miles.
—*Spillway* is 9.6 miles.
Note: The Eleven-Mile State Recreation Area is not accessible from this canyon.

The Windy-Ridge Bristlecone Pine Scenic Area is located four miles northwest of Alma.

Six campgrounds are located in the Eleven-Mile Canyon area, south of US 24 at Lake George. From the east side of town, turn south on Forest Road 240. Mileages to the following campgrounds are given from the junction of US 24 and Forest Road 240:
—*Blue Mountain* is 1.3 miles southwest; then left on Forest Road 240 for ½ mile.
—*Riverside* is 2½ miles.

Please notice that this little guy is actually grinning!

South Park Ranger District *(continued)*

Standing petrified sequoia stumps are displayed at the Florissant Fossil Beds National Monument. Hiking trails provide access to the back country of Pike National Forest.

Campgrounds	Elevation (feet)	Camp Units	Drinking Water	Toilets (V = vault)	Small Trailers	Fee Area (in season)
Aspen	9,900	12	X	V	X	X
Beaver Creek	10,900	3		V	X	
*Blue Mountain	8,200	21	X	V	X	X
Buffalo Springs	9,000	17	X	V	X	
Cove	8,400	5	X	V	X	X
Fourmile	10,600	14	X	V	X	X
Happy Meadows	7,900	6	X	V	X	X
Horseshoe	10,000	19	X	V	X	X
Jefferson Creek	10,100	17	X	V	X	X
Kite Lake	12,000	7		V		
Lodgepole	9,900	35	X	V	X	X
Lost Park	10,000	10	X	V	X	
Michigan Creek	10,000	13	X	V	X	X
Spillway	8,500	24	X	V	X	X
Riverside	8,000	19	X	V	X	X
Round Mountain	8,500	16	X	V	X	X
Selkirk	10,500	15	X	V	X	
Springer Gulch	8,300	15	X	V	X	X
Spruce Grove	8,600	28	X	V	X	X
Wagon Tongue	8,400	7		V	X	
Weston Pass	10,200	14	X	V	X	

* On MISTIX reservation system.

Three campgrounds are located in the Jefferson Creek area; access is gained by turning north onto Forest Road 400 from US 285 at Jefferson:
- —*Lodgepole* is reached by traveling 2 miles north on Forest Road 400, then right on Forest Road 401 for 2½ miles.
- —*Aspen* is approximately ½ mile beyond Lodgepole on Forest Road 401.
- —*Jefferson Creek* is 1 mile beyond Aspen Campground.

Michigan Creek—6 miles northwest of Jefferson on Forest Road 400.

Lost Park—also accessible from Jefferson. Go 1¼ miles northeast of Jefferson on US 285, then 19¾ miles southeast on Forest Road 127.

Selkirk Campground—northwest of Como. Take Forest Road 40 northwest for 3½ miles; then left on Forest Road 405 for less than 1 mile; then right on Forest Road 406 for 2 miles.

Six campgrounds are located in the area of Fairplay off of US 285.
- —*Beaver Creek* is north of US 285 at Fairplay; take Forest Road 413 north for 5 miles.
- —*Kite Lake* is northwest of Fairplay; take SH 9 northwest for 6 miles (past the small town of Alma); then left on Forest Road 416 for 6 miles.
- —*Horseshoe* is 1.3 miles south of Fairplay on US 285; then 7 miles west on Forest Road 421.
- —*Fourmile* is 1 mile beyond Horseshoe Campground on Forest Road 421.
- —*Weston Pass* is 5 miles south of Fairplay on US 285; then 11 miles southwest on Forest Road 425.
- —*Buffalo Springs* is 14½ miles south of Fairplay on US 285; then ½ mile west on Forest Road 431.

For Information

South Park Ranger District
P.O. Box 219
Fairplay, CO 80440
(719) 836-2031

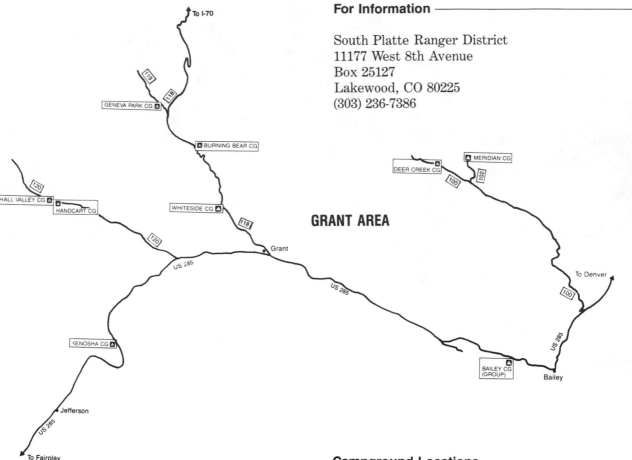

GRANT AREA

For Information

South Platte Ranger District
11177 West 8th Avenue
Box 25127
Lakewood, CO 80225
(303) 236-7386

Campground Locations

Eight campgrounds are located in the Grant area off of US 285:

—*Whiteside, Burning Bear,* and *Geneva Park* are all located northwest of Grant on Forest Road 118: Whiteside is 2½ miles; Burning Bear is 5¼ miles; and Geneva Park is 7 miles, then ¼ mile northwest on Forest Road 119.

—*Handcart* and *Hall Valley* are both northwest of Grant. Travel 3 miles west on US 285, then 5 miles northwest on Forest Road 120. The 2 campgrounds are less than ¼ mile from each other.

—*Kenosha Pass Campground* is 4¼ miles northeast of Jefferson on US 285.

—*Deer Creek* and *Meridian* campgrounds are both northwest of Bailey, with access via Forest Road 100, 2.4 miles north on US 285. Deer Creek is 8 miles northwest on Forest Road 100; Meridian is 6.6 miles northwest on Forest Road 100, then 1 mile north on Forest Road 102.

Does the song "In a cabin, in the woods" come to mind?

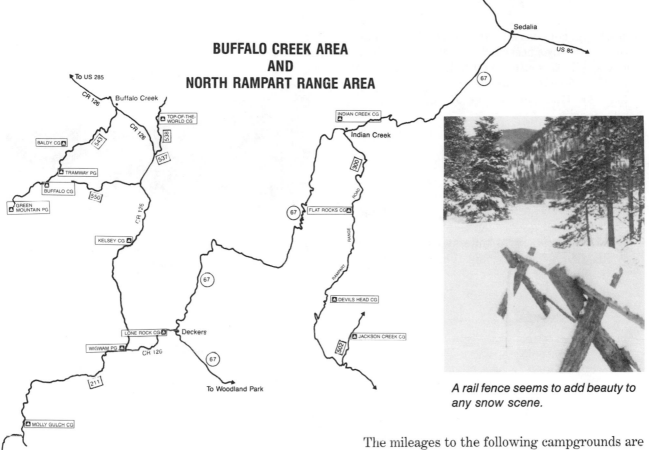

BUFFALO CREEK AREA
AND
NORTH RAMPART RANGE AREA

A rail fence seems to add beauty to any snow scene.

N. L. Gilchrest

This hunter is smiling—not because he has bagged his game, but because he has reached the 14,060-foot peak of Mt. Bierstadt.

Six campgrounds are located in the Buffalo Creek area. Access to Buffalo Creek is via an all-weather road (County Road 126) from US 285 on the north, and SH 67 at Deckers to the south.

The mileages to the following campgrounds are from Buffalo Creek:

—*Baldy* is 4 miles southeast on County Road 126, then southwest for 4 miles from the junction of County Road 126 and Forest Road 543.

—*Tramway* is 5 miles southwest from this junction.

—*Buffalo* is 5.7 miles southwest, then 1/4 mile east on Forest Road 550.

—*Green Mountain* is 7¾ miles southwest.

—*Kelsey* is 8 miles south on County Road 126.

—*Top-of-the-World Campground* is 2.7 miles southeast on County Road 126, then 1/4 mile southeast on Forest Road 537, then 1¼ miles north on Forest Road 538.

Wigwam and *Lone Rock* campgrounds are located near Deckers on County Road 126 from Buffalo Creek. Wigwam is near the junction of Forest Road 211 and County Road 126; Lone Rock is ½ mile west of Deckers.

Molly Gulch and *Goose Creek* campgrounds are both located southwest of Deckers. From the junction of County Road 126 and Forest Road 211, Molly Gulch is 9¼ miles and Goose Creek is 12 miles.

REGION 2

Pike National Forest 91

Four campgrounds are located in the North Rampart Range area accessible from US 85 at Sedalia via SH 67 southwest to the Indian Creek Junction. The junction of SH 67 with Forest Road 300 (Rampart Range Road) is 10 miles from Sedalia.

—*Indian Creek* is on SH 67, ¼ mile past the junction of Forest Road 300.

—*Flat Rocks* is 4.8 miles south on Forest Road 300.

—*Devils Head* is 9 miles south on Forest Road 300; then left after passing the Cabin Ridge Picnic area; go ¼ mile.

—*Jackson Creek* is 14 miles south on Forest Road 300; then 1½ miles northeast on Forest Road 502.

An abandoned miner's cabin has a way of giving a historic flavor to the backcountry.

Campgrounds	Elevation (feet)	Camp Units	Drinking Water	Toilets (V = vault)	Small Trailers	Fee Area (in season)
† Baldy	7,800	8	X	V		
*Buffalo	7,400	41	X	V	X	X
Burning Bear	9,500	13	X	V	X	
Deer Creek	9,000	13	X	V	X	X
Devils Head	8,800	22	X	V	X	X
Flat Rocks	8,200	20	X	V	X	X
Geneva Park	9,800	26	X	V	X	
Goose Creek	8,100	10	X	V	X	
Green Mountain	7,600	6	X	V		
Hall Valley	9,900	9	X	V	X	
Handcart	9,800	10	X	V		
Indian Creek	7,500	10	X	V	X	X
Jackson Creek	8,100	9	X	V	X	
Kelsey	8,000	17	X	V	X	
Kenosha Pass	10,000	25	X	V	X	X
*Lone Rock	6,400	19	X	V	X	X
Meridian	9,000	18	X	V	X	
Molly Gulch	7,500	15		V	X	
Top-of-the-World	7,500	7	X	V	X	
† Tramway	7,200	6	X	V		
Whiteside	8,900	5		V		
Wigwam	6,600	10	X	V	X	

* On MISTIX reservation system.
Group campgrounds: Bailey & Meadows.
† Tent camping only.

Pueblo State Recreation Area

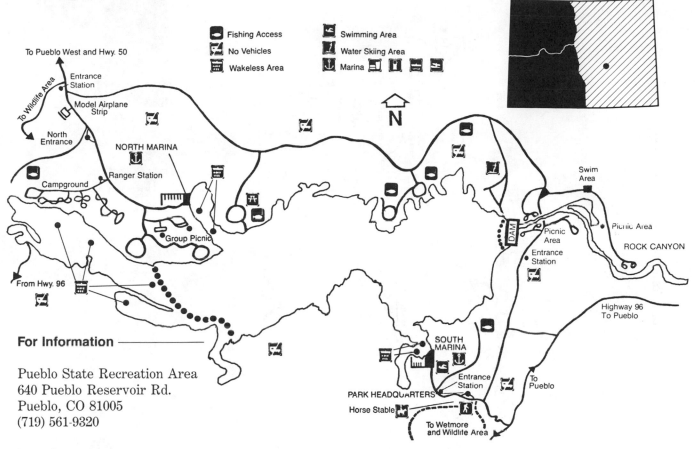

Fishing Access
No Vehicles
Wakeless Area
Swimming Area
Water Skiing Area
Marina

For Information

Pueblo State Recreation Area
640 Pueblo Reservoir Rd.
Pueblo, CO 81005
(719) 561-9320

Location

Pueblo State Recreation Area is located west of
I-25 at Pueblo, off of US 50. From Pueblo, go west
on US 50 for 4 miles; turn south on Pueblo Blvd.
and go 4 miles to Thatcher Ave.; turn west and go 6
miles. One of the state's most popular water sports
areas, this 17,035-acre park lies in a setting of contrast. The semi-arid plains around the reservoir appear to stretch endlessly eastward, while the
Greenhorn and Sangre de Cristo mountain ranges
form an alpine backdrop. Prickly pear and other
cacti are found here, along with cottonwoods and
willows. Limestone cliffs and flat-top buttes rim the
4,646-acre reservoir's irregular, 17-mile shoreline.
Elevation: 4,900 feet.

Facilities & Activities

214 campsites
electrical hookups
showers
dump station
laundry
group campground
visitor/nature center
picnic sites
group picnic area available
swimming
bathhouse
snackbar
boating
boat ramps
marina
boat rental
fishing
fish cleaning station
water skiing
sailboarding
sailboard rental
model airplane field
ice fishing
snow tubing
winter camping
18 miles of hiking trails
16 miles of bicycling trails
horseback riding

Rocky Mountain National Park

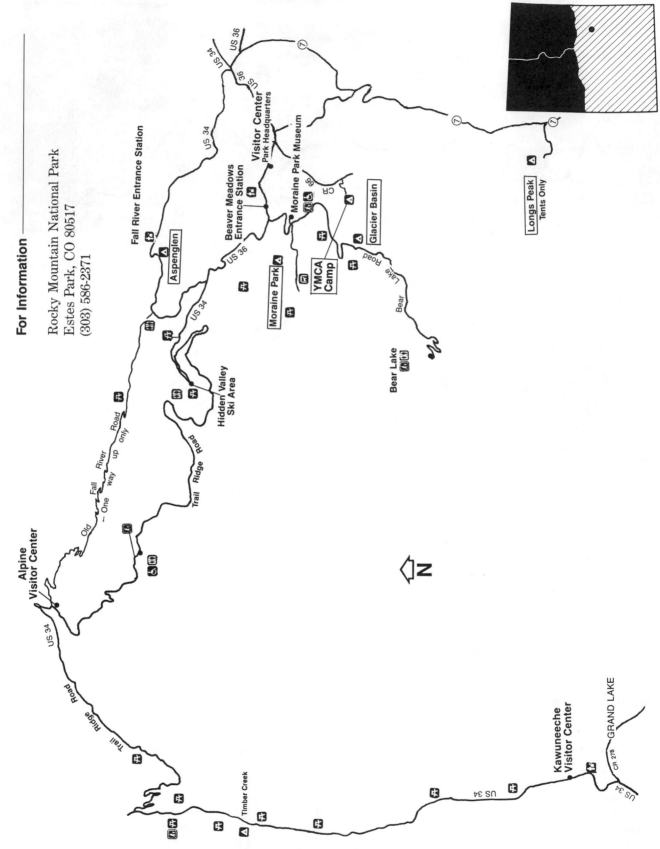

For Information

Rocky Mountain National Park
Estes Park, CO 80517
(303) 586-2371

Fall River Entrance Station

Aspenglen

Beaver Meadows
Entrance Station

Visitor Center
Park Headquarters

Moraine Park Museum

CR 66

Glacier Basin

Longs Peak
Tents Only

Moraine Park

YMCA
Camp

Bear Lake

Bear Lake Road

Hidden Valley
Ski Area

Trail Ridge Road

Old Fall River Road
— One way up only

Alpine
Visitor Center

US 34

US 36

US 34

US 43

US 36

Trail Ridge Road

Timber Creek

Kawuneeche
Visitor Center

GRAND LAKE

CR 278

US 34

N

Rocky Mountain National Park *(continued)*

Location

Rocky Mountain National Park's rich scenery typifies the massive grandeur of the Rocky Mountains. Elevations range from 8,200 feet to 14,255 feet in this 414 square-mile park. One-third of the park is above tree line. The park is accessible by Trail Ridge Road, which takes you 12,183 feet above sea level and crosses the Continental Divide. Access from the east is by US 34/36 and SH 7 to Estes Park, and from the southwest by US 40 to Granby, then US 34 to Grand Lake. Trail Ridge Road is usually closed from mid-October until Memorial Day; opening and closing dates vary depending on weather conditions. A feature of the park is the marked differences found with the changing elevation; the glacial landscape of the Rocky Mountains, with its valleys, highlands of pine, fir, and spruce forests, alpine meadows, clear streams and crystal lakes provides a broad spectrum of camping experiences.

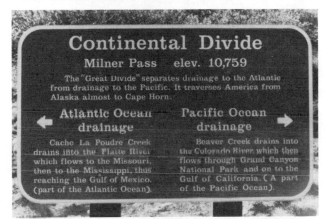

U.S. 34/Trail Ridge Road crosses the Continental Divide at Milner Pass.

Trail Ridge Road has numerous overlooks where travelers can enjoy the views and read the interpretive displays.

50-mile scenic drive on Trail Ridge Road
downhill skiing (Hidden Valley)
cross-country skiing
snowshoeing
winter mountaineering

Longs Peak Trail

The main hiking trail to the park's highest peak (14,255 feet) leads through subalpine forests, tundra, and glacial landscapes. For those who are not technical climbers but would like the experience of reaching a mountain top, Longs Peak is the answer. In July, August and most of September, the route through the Keyhole can be negotiated without technical climbing equipment. The north and east faces are for technical climbing only. The Longs Peak Trailhead is off of SH 7.

Recreational Activities

camping
backcountry camping
picnicking
355 miles of hiking trails
self-guiding trails
horseback riding
fishing
mountain climbing
campfire talks
ranger-guided walks
wayside exhibits

Campgrounds	Elevation (feet)	Number of Sites	Reservations	Modern Restrooms	Trailer Dump Station	Amphitheater	Public Telephones
Moraine Park	8,150	247	X	X	X	X	X
Glacier Basin	8,600	150	X	X	X	X	X
Glacier Basin Group		12	X	X	X	X	X
Longs Peak	9,400	28		X			
Aspenglen	8,230	61		X		X	X
Timber Creek	8,900	100		X	X	X	X

Rocky Mountain National Park *(continued)*

The lengthy climb up Longs Peak is demanding. The elevation gain is 4,700 feet, and the 16-mile round trip can take 12 hours. Be sure you are acclimated to high elevations before you try this rigorous trip. To avoid afternoon lightning storms around the summit, start before 6 a.m. and be in good physical condition. Even in summer the weather can suddenly turn cold, so carry wool sweaters, spare socks, mittens, rain gear, and lunch. For information about Longs Peak, call the ranger station, (303) 586-4975.

Bear Lake is a popular day-use area; a hiking trail encircles the lake and the Bear Lake trailhead provides access to several trails in the area.

Campground Locations

Moraine Park—3 miles west of park headquarters/visitor center on the Bear Lake Road.

Glacier Basin—9 miles west of Estes Park on the Bear Lake Road.

Longs Peak—11 miles south of Estes Park and 1 mile west off of SH 7, at Longs Peak trailhead.

Aspenglen—5 miles west of Estes Park near the Fall River Entrance Station.

Timbercreek—10 miles north of Grand Lake on the Trail Ridge Road.

General Park Information

▲ There are 3 visitor centers:
  Park Headquarters—on east side; open all year; (303) 586-2371
  Alpine—on Trail Ridge Road; open June through September
  Kawuneeche—on west side; open all year; (303) 627-3471
▲ There are 598 campsites at the 6 campgrounds.

▲ Moraine Park and Glacier Basin Campgrounds are on the TICKETRON reservation system from the end of June through mid-August.
▲ 3 campgrounds (*Aspenglen, Longs Peak, & Timber Creek*) are open year-round on first-come basis. Longs Peak and Timber Creek are not plowed, so once the snows begin you have to carry supplies to your campsite.
▲ None of the campgrounds have water in winter; no campground fees are charged if water is unavailable.
▲ There is a 7-day camping limit parkwide (June 1 through September 30) except at Longs Peak (3-day limit).
▲ 15 additional days are permitted parkwide October 1 through May 31. Camping is permitted only in designated areas.
▲ RV's can be accommodated in all campgrounds, except Longs Peak, which is a tents-only campground.
▲ Comfort stations (sink and flush toilets in summer), piped water, and trash receptacles are available at campgrounds.
▲ Reservations are required for the use of the group campground at Glacier Basin. This campground is for "organized" non-profit groups.
▲ *Handicamp* is a backcountry camping area specifically designed for the disabled. It will accommodate 10 campers and a maximum of 5 wheelchair users. Phone (303) 586-2371 for details.
▲ A backcountry use permit is required if you spend the night in the backcountry. The free permit may be obtained in advance or upon arrival at the backcountry office at park headquarters, the Kawuneeche Visitor Center, and at most ranger stations.
▲ Those attempting technical climbs should be familiar with the park's climbing regulations.
▲ The only bears in the park are black bears; there are no grizzlies.
▲ Campfire programs are conducted nightly in campground amphitheaters during the summer.
▲ Pets are permitted in the campgrounds provided they are on a leash or under physical control; they are not permitted on trails.
▲ There are no service stations within the park.
▲ A full range of services is available outside the park at Estes Park on the east and at Grand Lake on the west.

Roosevelt National Forest

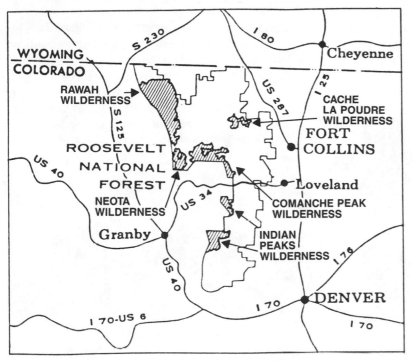

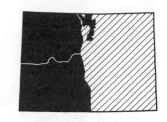

For Information

Arapaho and Roosevelt National
   Forest Headquarters
240 West Prospect Road
Fort Collins, CO 80526
(303) 498-1100

Location

Roosevelt National Forest, located on the eastern side of the Rockies, was named in honor of the man most responsible for creating the National Park System. Originally part of Medicine Bow Forest Reserve established in 1897, it became the Colorado National Forest in 1910. Then in 1932 President Herbert Hoover renamed the forest in honor of President Theodore Roosevelt. There are five wilderness areas within the 788,333-acre Roosevelt National Forest. These areas provide opportunities for solitude and primitive recreation with trail access only.

Wilderness Areas

Cache La Poudre Wilderness, is a 9,400-acre wilderness characterized by steep, rugged terrain along the Pourdre River and the Little South Fork of the Poudre. Elevations range from 6,200 feet to 8,600 feet, and the area is accessible most of the year. The Mt. McConnel National Recreation Trail is the only maintained trail in this wilderness. Travel is accomplished by scrambling and bushwhacking in stream bottoms, on ridges, and along game trails. A rugged and challenging wilderness experience is available in this sloping and seldom traveled area.

Incredible beauty abounds in the backcountry

REGION 2

Roosevelt National Forest   97

R. Tatum

. . . trails like this can lead you there . . . either for a day . . .

Comanche Peak Wilderness, named for the prominent 12,702-foot peak, is a 67,000-acre wilderness that features lodgepole and spruce-fir forests below expanses of alpine tundra. Many scenic trails provide access to this area that borders the north side of Rocky Mountain National Park. Elevations range from 8,000 to 12,700 feet.

Neota Wilderness has 9,890 acres. The dominant features are large flat-top ridges formed by erosion and glacial action. Elevations range from 10,000 to 11,800 feet. About one-third of the land inside the wilderness boundary is covered by alpine tundra and barren rock faces. Below the tundra, a spruce-fir forest is dominant. Along the Neota and Corral creeks, wet meadow areas predominate. This wilderness area is not a high use area and therefore provides good opportunities for solitude, fishing, and wildlife viewing.

Rawah Wilderness is a 76,394-acre area located on the east side of the Medicine Bow Mountains.

Elevations range from 8,400 to 13,000 feet. The lower country is dominated by dense stands of lodgepole pine, while progressively higher elevations are covered by spruce-fir forests, alpine tundra, and barren rock formations. The high peaks were carved by glaciers, resulting in spectacular cirque lakes and moraines. There are 25 named lakes, ranging in size from 5 to 39 acres.

. . . or for an extended period of time.

Indian Peaks Wilderness is located primarily within the Arapaho and Roosevelt national forests, although the northernmost portion is located in Rocky Mountain National Park. The name Indian Peaks was selected because many of the peaks within the Wilderness are named for Indian tribes in the West. This 73,391-acre wilderness contains vast areas of alpine tundra, numerous cirque basins with remnant glaciers, and nearly 50 lakes in the shadows of the Continental Divide. Elevations range from 8,400 to 13,000 feet. This is the most frequently visited wilderness in Colorado.

This fisherman accommodated the photographer by displaying one of his "keepers" for the day.

Boulder Ranger District

Campground Locations

Kelly Dahl—3 miles south of Nederland on SH 119.

Rainbow Lakes—6½ miles north of Nederland on SH 72; then turn at sign saying "Mountain Research Station" and go 5 miles on a bumpy gravel/dirt road.

Pawnee—turn west on County Road 102 (Brainard Lake) off of SH 72 at Ward; travel 5 miles.

Peaceful Valley and *Camp Dick* campgrounds—both are northwest of Boulder off of SH 72 at town of Peaceful Valley; travel ¼ mile west of town on Forest Road 92 for Peaceful Valley Campground; Camp Dick is just ¾ mile beyond on Forest Road 92.

Olive Ridge—15 miles south of Estes Park or 1½ miles north of Allenspark on SH 7.

Into each life some rain must fall!

For Information

Boulder Ranger District
2995 Baseline Rd., Room 110
Boulder, CO 80303
(303) 444-6001

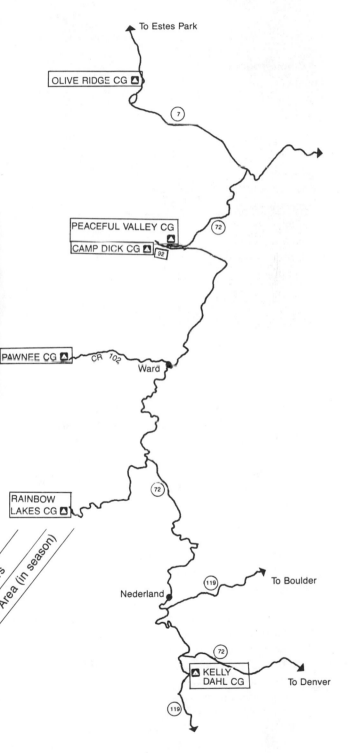

Campgrounds	Elevation (feet)	Camp Units	Drinking Water	Toilets (V = vault)	Small Trailers	Fee Area (in season)
Camp Dick	8,600	34	X	V	X	X
Kelly Dahl	8,600	46	X	V	X	X
*Olive Ridge	8,400	56	X	V	X	X
Pawnee	10,400	55	X	V	X	X
Peaceful Valley	8,500	15	X	V	X	X
Rainbow Lakes	10,000	18		V		

* On MISTIX reservation system.

Estes-Poudre Ranger District

For Information

Estes-Poudre Ranger District
148 Remington Street
Fort Collins, CO 80524
(303) 482-3822

Many parks offer ranger programs during the summer.

Colorado Division of Parks and Outdoor Recreation

Campgrounds	Elevation (feet)	Camp Units	Drinking Water	Toilets (V = vault)	Small Trailers	Fee Area (in season)
Ansel Watrous	5,800	19	X	V	X	X
**Big Bend	7,600	9	X	V		X
Buckhorn Canyon	8,000	10			X	
Crown Point-Pingree	8,000	12			X	
Kelly Flats	6,800	23	X	V	X	X
Mishawaka	5,800	3		V	X	
*Mountain Park	6,700	45	X	V	X	X
Narrows Coop	6,500	4		V	X	
Sleeping Elephant	7,900	15	X	V	X	X
Stevens Gulch	6,000	4		V	X	
Stove Prairie Landing	6,000	7		V	X	
Tom Bennett	9,000	12		V	X	
Tunnel Rest Area	7,900	2		V	X	
**Upper Landing	6,000	5		V		

* On MISTIX reservation system.
** Walk-in camping.

Campground Locations

Eleven campgrounds are located along SH 14 that parallels the Cache Poudre River; from Fort Collins, take US 287 northwest to Laramie, WY, SH 14 forks left at the little town of Teds Place:

—*Mishawaka* is 22 miles west of Fort Collins.
—*Ansel Watrous* is 23 miles.
—*Stove Prairie Landing* is 26 miles.
—*Upper Landing* is 27 miles.
—*Stevens Gulch* is 27 miles.
—*Narrows Coop* is 30 miles.
—*Mountain Park* is 33 miles.
—*Kelly Flats* is 37 miles.
—*Big Bend* is 49 miles.
—*Sleeping Elephant* is 53 miles.
—*Tunnel Rest Area* is 55 miles west of Fort Collins.

Buckhorn Canyon Campground—located on Buckhorn Canyon Road between SH 14 and Masonville. From SH 14 the road junction is just east of the Stove Prairie Landing Campground; go south for 10 miles. From Masonville, the campground is approximately 14 miles northwest.

Crown Point-Pingree—on Pingree Park Road (Forest Road 131) south of SH 14. From SH 14 the road junction is between Eggers Rest Area and Kelly Flats Campground; turn south and go 8 miles.

Tom Bennett—beyond Crown Point-Pingree Campground an additional 3 miles on Forest Road 131, then 5 miles on Forest Road 145.

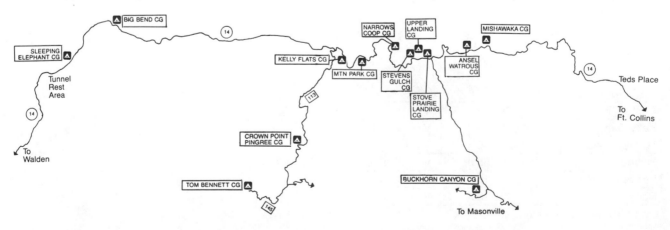

These backcountry users have an opportunity to practice the rules of "low impact" suggested by the National Forest Service.

The view of Lake Granby, from the Stillwater Campground in the Arapaho National Recreation Area, is still quite breathtaking, even when the water level is low (see page 67).

Winter camping in the beautiful Maroon Bells-Snowmass Wilderness, one of 25 designated wilderness areas in Colorado located in the national forests (see page 56).

The Durango and Silverton Narrow Gauge Railroad offers breathtaking views of the Animas river gorge.

There are no signs of civilization evident in this magnificent wilderness.

True wilderness areas are accessible only by trails.

Base camp for climbing the 14,191-foot Crestone Needle in the Rio Grande and San Isabel National Forests (see pages 135 and 141).

Tent camping is quite popular in Colorado; no doubt, this roomy tent houses an entire family.

These campers are probably lulled to sleep each night by the sound of the river.

This snow shelter, called a quinzhee, will accommodate two persons.

103

. . . just getting a better view of the scenery near Lizard Head Pass south of Telluride.

Many state parks and national parks offer opportunities for horseback riding.

Return to this scene in the fall and these aspen trees will be a vivid yellow.

Rustic, primitive cabins are available on a rental basis at North Michigan Reservoir at Colorado State Forest (see page 31).

Notice the well organized "kitchen" at this campsite.

An interesting place to pitch a tent—in fact, it may be the only available place in sight!

Colorado rivers offer mountain scenery and access to rugged canyons. Rafts are most often used; river trips range from a couple of hours to a week or more.

The quaking aspen is quite a contrast to the Colorado blue spruce, the official state tree.

M. Little

Lory State Park offers 20 miles of mountain bike trails (see page 83).

M. Little

T. Gilchrest

These hikers are dwarfed by magnificent mountains and towering trees.

. . . just to remind you that summer isn't the only camping season in Colorado.

M. Little

The incredible Hanging Lake, precariously perched on a mountain ledge and reached via a steep 1¾-mile trail is truly a sight to behold. Access is from I-70, 10 miles east of Glenwood Springs.

T. Gilchrest

Words to describe this scene at Snowmass Lake would only detract from its beauty!

C. Thornton

Chambers Lake is typical of numerous mountain lakes in that it is accessible via hiking trails from nearby forest campgrounds.

M. Little

Highline State Recreation Area, a city-like park in a rural setting, has beautiful trees and a 174 surface-acre lake for boating, fishing, and water skiing (see page 34).

M. Little

You can get lots of thinking done when the fish aren't biting!

Maroon Lake, southwest of Aspen, is an access point to the Maroon Bells-Snowmass Wilderness Area (see page 56).

Windsurfing is a growing sport for Colorado campers, and no wonder with all the lakes and reservoirs in the state!

The backroads of Colorado are special places when trees are arrayed in their fall foliage.

Redfeather Ranger District

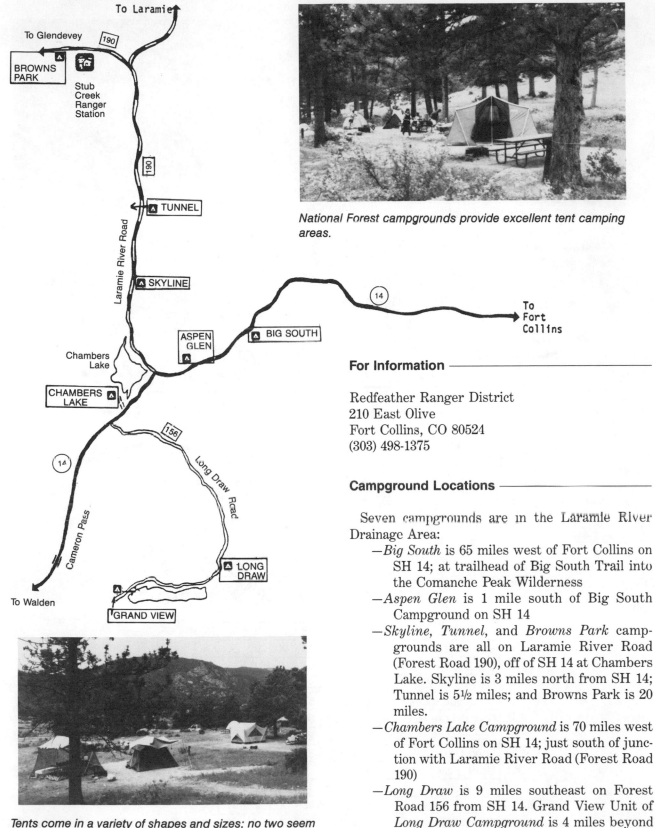

National Forest campgrounds provide excellent tent camping areas.

Tents come in a variety of shapes and sizes; no two seem to be alike.

For Information

Redfeather Ranger District
210 East Olive
Fort Collins, CO 80524
(303) 498-1375

Campground Locations

Seven campgrounds are in the Laramie River Drainage Area:

—*Big South* is 65 miles west of Fort Collins on SH 14; at trailhead of Big South Trail into the Comanche Peak Wilderness

—*Aspen Glen* is 1 mile south of Big South Campground on SH 14

—*Skyline, Tunnel,* and *Browns Park* campgrounds are all on Laramie River Road (Forest Road 190), off of SH 14 at Chambers Lake. Skyline is 3 miles north from SH 14; Tunnel is 5½ miles; and Browns Park is 20 miles.

—*Chambers Lake Campground* is 70 miles west of Fort Collins on SH 14; just south of junction with Laramie River Road (Forest Road 190)

—*Long Draw* is 9 miles southeast on Forest Road 156 from SH 14. Grand View Unit of *Long Draw Campground* is 4 miles beyond on Long Draw Reservoir.

Redfeather Ranger District *(continued)*

Five campgrounds are located in the vicinity of the town of Red Feather Lakes, accessible via Forest Road 162 from SH 14 at Rustic or from The Forks on US 287:

—*Dowdy Lake South Shore* and *West Shore* campgrounds are 1½ miles east of the village of Red Feather Lakes on Forest Road 218.

—*West Lake* is on Red Feather Lakes Road, 2 miles east of Red Feather Lakes on Forest Road 200.

—*Bellaire Lake* is 5 miles south of Red Feather Lakes on Forest Road 162.

—*North Fork Poudre* is 7 miles west of Red Feather Lakes on Forest Road 162.

It's a thrill to catch them—whatever the size!

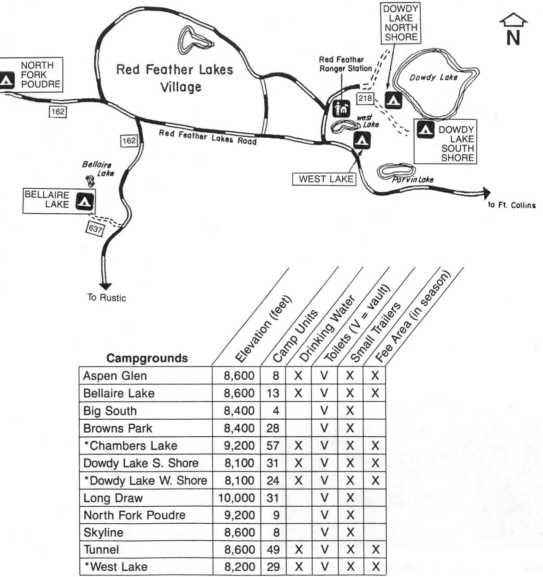

Campgrounds	Elevation (feet)	Camp Units	Drinking Water	Toilets (V = vault)	Small Trailers	Fee Area (in season)
Aspen Glen	8,600	8	X	V	X	X
Bellaire Lake	8,600	13	X	V	X	X
Big South	8,400	4		V	X	
Browns Park	8,400	28		V	X	
*Chambers Lake	9,200	57	X	V	X	X
Dowdy Lake S. Shore	8,100	31	X	V	X	X
*Dowdy Lake W. Shore	8,100	24	X	V	X	X
Long Draw	10,000	31		V	X	
North Fork Poudre	9,200	9		V	X	
Skyline	8,600	8		V	X	
Tunnel	8,600	49	X	V	X	X
*West Lake	8,200	29	X	V	X	X

* On MISTIX reservation system.

San Isabel National Forest

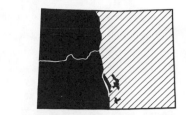

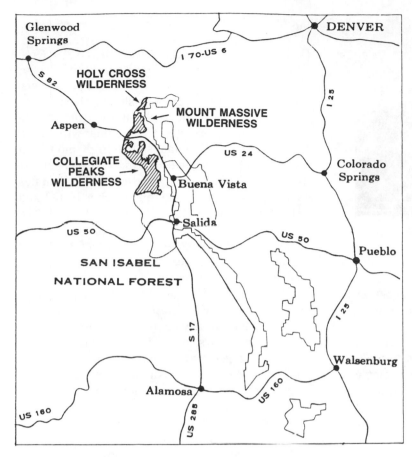

Inner-tube fishing is one answer to the wake-less boating requirement.

For Information

Pike and San Isabel National Forest Headquarters
1920 Valley Drive
Pueblo, CO 81008
(719) 545-8737

The Spanish Peaks are among the most important historic landmarks of the southwest.

Location

San Isabel National Forest encompasses 1,237,920 acres and has the highest average elevation of any national forest. Elevations range from 6,000 feet to the highest peak in Colorado, the 14,433-foot Mt. Elbert, one of 17 mountain peaks 14,000 feet and over in this forest.

Special Notes

The high mountain peaks of the Sangre de Cristo Range, the Spanish Peaks, the Collegiate Peaks, and the Sawatch Range offer some outstanding scenic beauty. For the expert and novice climber, these mountains offer some challenging and rewarding effort. The 14,421-foot Mt. Massive is the second highest peak in Colorado. Both Mt. Massive and Mt. Elbert can be climbed by those with no mountain climbing experience. Trails lead to the summits of both peaks; one full day should be allowed for ascent and return.

J. A. Gebert

The Spanish Peaks are clearly visible from Lathrop State Park, west of I-25 at Walsenburg.

The Spanish Peaks, near La Veta, are important landmarks of the Southwest. Their isolated location and abrupt rise of 7,000 feet above the Great Plains made them of special significance to Indian tribes, Spanish explorers, and American frontiersmen. The Great Dikes are among the unusual geologic features of the Spanish Peaks; they radiate out from the mountains like spokes of a wheel. These walls are spectacular in height and length. A scenic drive around the Peaks offers outstanding photographic opportunities.

Wilderness Areas

Collegiate Peaks Wilderness covers 159,900 acres in 3 national forests: Gunnison, White River, and San Isabel. The area contains 8 peaks over 14,000 feet high. Climbers should consult reliable guidebooks and seek advice from knowledgeable climbers who are familiar with these peaks. Timberline lakes and high mountain streams offer excellent fishing and scenery.

Holy Cross Wilderness, located about 10 miles northwest of Leadville, on the San Isabel and the White River national forests lies astride the Continental Divide. It was named for the widely known 14,005-foot Mount of the Holy Cross. The wilderness contains numerous high peaks along with scenic basins and valleys dotted with small natural lakes near timberline.

Mount Massive Wilderness near Leadville, along the Continental Divide, is dominated by and includes Colorado's second highest peak, Mt. Massive at 14,421 feet elevation. The wilderness joins the White River National Forest's Hunter Fryingpan Wilderness along the Continental Divide. The area is characterized by alpine mountains and ridges sloping off the spruce-fir and lodgepole pine forests at lower elevations. High mountain lakes are numerous.

This large mushroom-looking tent surely must allow you to stand up while dressing!

San Carlos Ranger District

For Information

San Carlos Ranger District
326 Dozier Street
Canon City, CO 81212
(719) 275-4119

Campground Locations

Alvarado is southwest of Westcliffe. Travel 3½ miles south on SH 69, then 5 miles west on Schoolfield Road, then 1 mile southwest on Forest Road 302.

Cuchara, Blue Lake, Bear Lake, and *Purgatoire* campgrounds are all located in the Spanish Peaks area, southwest of LaVeta, accessible from SH 12 through Cuchara:

—*Cuchara Campground* is 3½ miles south of Cuchara on SH 12.
—*Blue Lake* is 3½ miles south of Cuchara, then west on Forest Road 413 for 3½ miles.
—*Bear Lake* is 1 mile past Blue Lake on Forest Road 413.
—*Purgatoire* is 13½ miles south of Cuchara on SH 12, then 3 miles west on Forest Road 411.

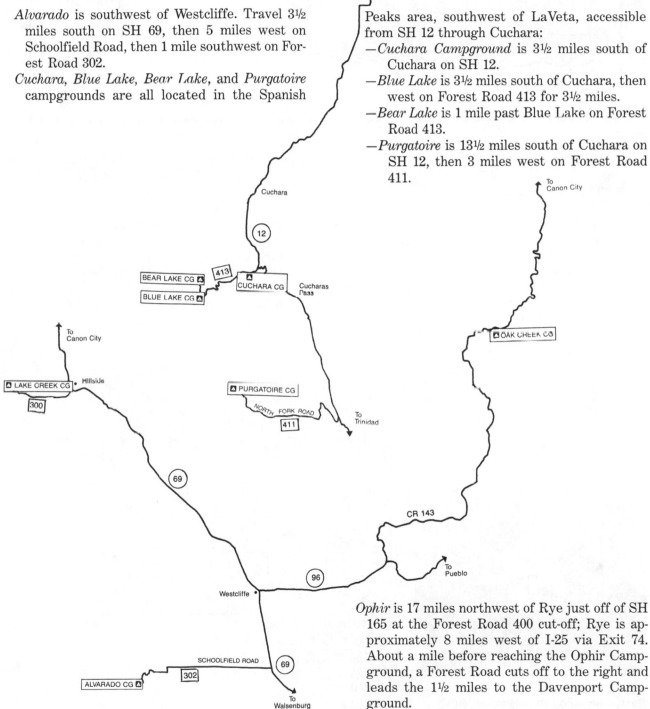

Ophir is 17 miles northwest of Rye just off of SH 165 at the Forest Road 400 cut-off; Rye is approximately 8 miles west of I-25 via Exit 74. About a mile before reaching the Ophir Campground, a Forest Road cuts off to the right and leads the 1½ miles to the Davenport Campground.

REGION 2

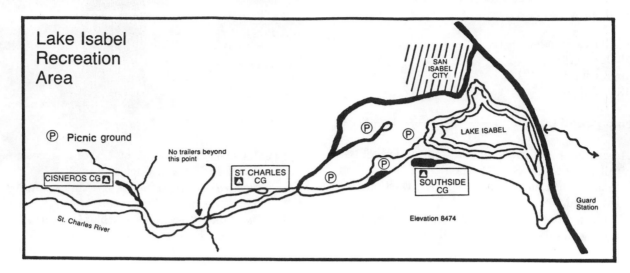

Lake Isabel
Recreation
Area

Ⓟ Picnic ground

No trailers beyond this point

CISNEROS CG ▲

ST CHARLES CG ▲

SOUTHSIDE CG

SAN ISABEL CITY

LAKE ISABEL

Ⓟ

Ⓟ

Ⓟ

Ⓟ

Guard Station

Elevation 8474

St. Charles River

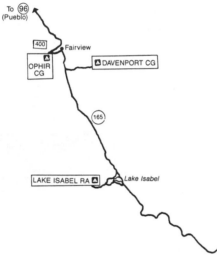

To ⑨⑥ (Pueblo)

④⓪⓪   Fairview

OPHIR CG ▲

▲ DAVENPORT CG

①⑥⑤

LAKE ISABEL RA ▲   Lake Isabel

Rye   ①⑥⑤   To I-70

Lake Isabel Recreation Area has 3 campgrounds: *Southside, St. Charles,* and *Cisneros*. The recreation area is on the St. Charles River, 10 miles northwest of Rye on SH 165; take Forest Road 308 to reach the campgrounds.

Lake Creek is 3 miles west of the town of Hillside on Forest Road 300; Hillside is on SH 69, south of US 50 between Salida and Canon City.

Oak Creek is located 12 miles south of Canon City on County Road 143. The campground is located next to the Oak Creek Group Area.

Campgrounds	Elevation (feet)	Camp Units	Drinking Water	Toilets (V = vault)	Small Trailers	Fee Area (in season)
Alvarado	9,000	47	X	V	X	X
Bear Lake	10,500	15	X	V	X	X
Blue Lake	10,700	15	X	V	X	X
Cuchara	9,500	25	X	V	X	
Davenport	8,500	15	X	V	X	X
Lake Creek	8,300	11	X	V	X	X
Lake Isabel (Southside)	8,800	8	X	V	X	X
Lake Isabel (Cisneros)	8,800	25	X	V		X
Lake Isabel (St. Charles)	8,800	15	X	V	X	X
*Oak Creek	7,600	6	X	V		
Ophir	8,900	31	X	V		X
Purgatoire	9,700	23	X	V	X	

N. L. Gilchrest

A climber pauses near the summit of Blanca Peak; Ellingwood Peak is to the left.

* Also has a group campground; reservations required.

Trinidad State Recreation Area

Facilities & Activities

62 campsites
electrical hookups
showers
dump station
laundry
picnic sites
group picnic area available
boating
boat ramps
fishing
water skiing
sailboarding
cross-country skiing
ice skating
ice fishing
snow tubing
winter camping
2 nature trails
7 miles of hiking trails
4 miles of horseback trails

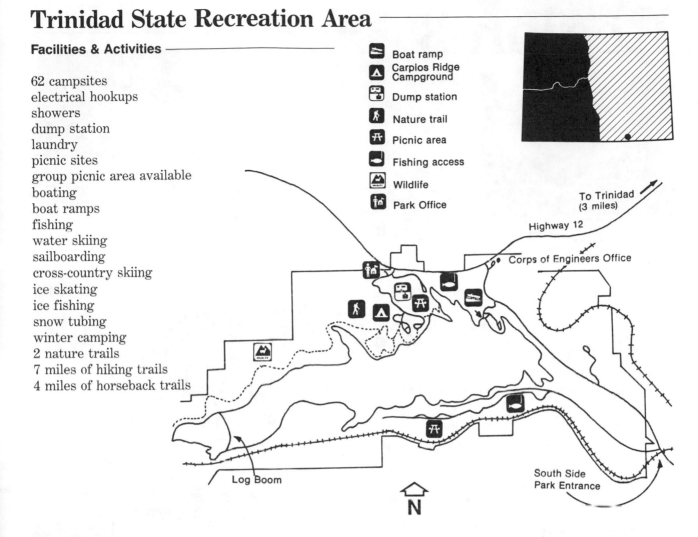

Boat ramp	
Carplos Ridge Campground	
Dump station	
Nature trail	
Picnic area	
Fishing access	
Wildlife	
Park Office	

To Trinidad
(3 miles)

Highway 12

Corps of Engineers Office

Log Boom

South Side
Park Entrance

N

For Information

Trinidad State Recreation Area
32610 Hwy. 12
Trinidad, CO 81082
(719) 846-6951

Location

Trinidad State Recreation Area lies in the Purgatorie River Valley west of Trinidad. To reach the park, travel 3 miles west on SH 12 from Exit 13 on I-25. The dam that created the 800-acre Trinidad Lake was built as an irrigation and flood control project by the U.S. Army Corps of Engineers. Several hiking/nature trails explore the 700-acre backcountry; total land acres are 1,500. For travelers entering or leaving the state via I-25, this is an excellent stop-over. At an elevation of 6,300 feet the park has great climate, good fishing, and is an uncrowded water sports paradise.

When entering or leaving the state via I-25, Trinidad is an excellent camping stopover.

Region 3

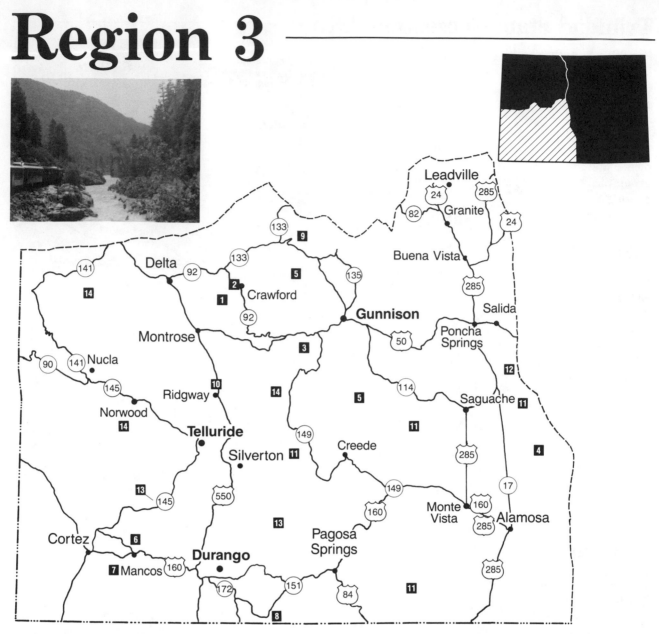

Black Canyon of the Gunnison National Monument

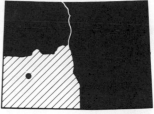

For Information

Black Canyon of the Gunnison National Monument
P.O. Box 1648
Montrose, CO 81402
(303) 240-6522

Location

Black Canyon of the Gunnison National Monument is located 15 miles east of Montrose. The south rim is reached via US 50 and SH 347; from Montrose, the north rim is reached by either US 50 east and SH 92 west through Curecanti National Recreation Area to Crawford, or US 50 northwest and SH 92 east through Delta to Crawford. From Crawford, a graveled county road goes to the north rim. The first route to the north rim is 90 miles and the second is 80 miles. Access to the north rim is closed in winter by snow. The south rim is open year-round, but is closed occasionally in winter due to heavy snows.

The main camping areas are located at an elevation of about 8,200 feet near the rim of the Black Canyon, an 1,800-foot-deep, dark gorge that has been carved by the Gunnison River. The canyon is 53 miles long, but only the deepest, most spectacular 12 miles of the gorge lie within the National Monument. No other canyon in North America combines the depth, narrowness, and sheerness of the Black Canyon of the Gunnison. The park has 20,762 acres, with 11,180 acres designated as wilderness area.

Both the south and north rim have numerous overlooks that enable visitors spectacular views of the canyon.

This overlook is on the south rim across from the Painted Wall.

REGION 3

Facilities & Activities

103 campsites at south rim
14 campsites at north rim
campgrounds have water but it should be used sparingly
12 backcountry campsites (free permit required)
all campsites are first-come, first-served
campgrounds are open mid-April through mid-November
picnic areas
South Rim Drive, a scenic auto tour with numerous overlooks
hiking trails & nature trails from overlooks

Rim House, the visitor center at south rim, has snack bar and souvenirs (open seasonally)
interpretive exhibits
seasonal ranger programs
rock climbing for experienced climbers (must register with rangers)

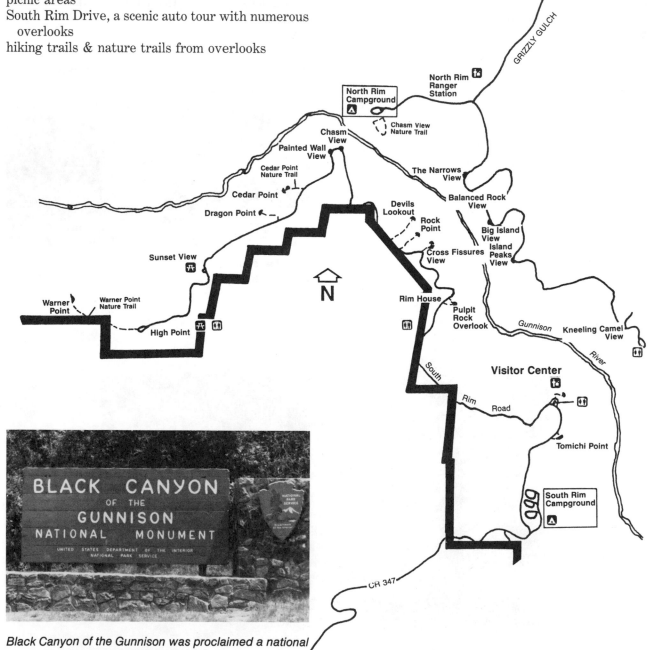

Black Canyon of the Gunnison was proclaimed a national monument in 1933 by President Hoover.

Crawford State Recreation Area

For Information

Crawford State Recreation Area
P.O. Box 147
Crawford, CO 81415
(303) 921-5721

Dam

To Crawford (1 mile)

To Black Canyon

N

Colo. Hwy. 92

To Black Mesa

LEGEND

🎇 Picnicking — — — Park Boundary

🔺 Camping

🚻 Comfort Station ▓ Swim Area

👥 Park Office

🚤 Boat Ramp

🗑 Dump Station

Location

Crawford State Recreation Area is located 1 mile south of Crawford and 14 miles north of the Black Canyon of the Gunnison National Monument. The 821-acre park may be reached from US 50 at Delta by traveling east on SH 92 to Hotchkiss, then south on SH 92 to Crawford. A 406-acre reservoir, built in 1963 by the US Bureau of Reclamation, is within the park boundaries. The park's 6,600-foot elevation guarantees visitors a mild climate at any season in the midst of rural Colorado where farms and ranches still surround the park.

These youngsters were eager to show the "trophy" cat-fish they just caught at Crawford State Recreation Area.

Facilities & Activities

55 campsites
dump station
picnic sites
group picnic area available
swimming
boating
boat ramps
fishing
water skiing
sailboarding
snowmobiling
cross-country skiing
ice skating
ice fishing
snow tubing
winter camping
horseback riding

Curecanti National Recreation Area

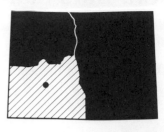

For Information

Curecanti National Recreation Area
102 Elk Creek
Gunnison, CO 81230
(303) 641-0406

Location

Curecanti National Recreation Area, located adjacent to and east of the Black Canyon of the Gunnison National Monument, is a 42,000-acre recreation area surrounded by mountains and encompassing three lakes—Blue Mesa, Morrow Point, and Crystal. The lakes were created by three dams on the Gunnison River, constructed to provide irrigation and hydroelectric power. These lakes extend for 40 miles along the Gunnison River. When full, Blue Mesa Lake, with a surface of 14 square miles and a 96-mile shoreline, is the largest lake in Colorado. The elevation is mostly above 7,500 feet.

There are two marinas on Blue Mesa Reservoir; this one at Lake Fork is located near the dam.

Special Notes

Elk Creek serves as park headquarters. Slide presentations and exhibits may be viewed at the Elk Creek Visitor Center, located 16 miles west of Gunnison off of US 50. The center is open from mid-May to late September; it is also open intermittently the rest of the year. Information stations are found at Lake Fork, Cimarron, and East Portal. Curecanti has over 400 campsites at a variety of drive-in, boat-in, and hike-in campgrounds for RVs and tents. Campgrounds remain open until closed by snow or freezing temperatures that sometimes dip as low as − 40° F. Generally, sites are accessible at Elk Creek year-round and at Lake Fork and Cimarron from mid-April through mid-November. Curecanti has no campsite reservation system except for organized group camping.

Recreational Activities

camping
picnicking
power boating
water skiing
sailing
windsurfing
fishing
7 developed hiking trails totaling 24 miles
horseback riding
ice fishing
cross-country skiing
snowmobiling
boat tours of Morrow Point Lake
scenic drive along SH 92
seasonal campfire programs

When full, Blue Mesa Lake has a 96-mile shoreline and is the largest lake in Colorado.

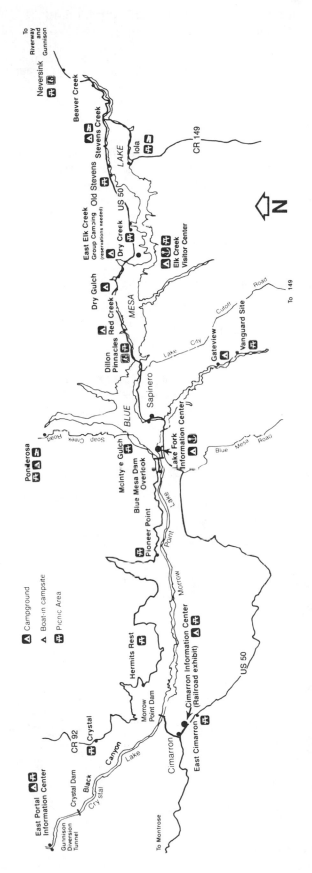

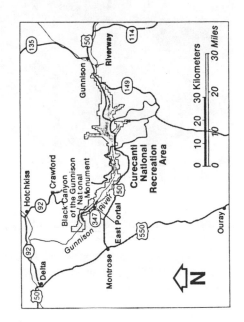

This overlook has a view of Morrow Point Lake—one of the three lakes created by dams on the Gunnison River.

REGION 3

Curecanti National Recreation Area *(continued)*

Visitors to Morrow Point Dam can view this railroad exhibit and take a self-guided tour.

Location of Major Developed Campgrounds

Cimarron—20 miles east of Montrose on US 50
Lake Fork—27 miles west of Gunnison on US 50
Elk Creek—16 miles west of Gunnison on US 50
Stevens Creek—12 miles west of Gunnison on US 50

Note: Lake Fork, Elk Creek, and Stevens Creek campgrounds are located close to Blue Mesa Lake in treeless, sagebrush, mesa country. Cimarron Campground, on the banks of Cimarron Creek, is more sheltered.

Location of Campgrounds with Limited Facilities

East Portal—2 miles below Crystal Dam at the bottom of the Black Canyon. Access via SH 347, 6 miles north of junction with US 50. Proceed 5 miles down East Portal Road.

Ponderosa—northwest end of the Soap Creek Arm of Blue Mesa Lake. Access via SH 92, ½ mile west of Blue Mesa Dam. Proceed north 7 miles on the Soap Creek gravel road. The road is very muddy and hazardous after a rain. Campsites are among scattered pine trees.

Gateview—extreme south end of the Lake Fork Arm of Blue Mesa Lake. Access via SH 149, 7 miles west of Powderhorn. Proceed north 6 miles on an improved narrow gravel road. Campsites are located near a deep, narrow canyon.

Red Creek—just north of US 50, 19 miles west of Gunnison.

Dry Gulch—just north of US 50, 17 miles west of Gunnison.

East Elk Creek (Group Campground)—just north of US 50, 16½ miles west of Gunnison.

Note: East Portal, Red Creek, Dry Gulch, and East Elk campgrounds are located among large cottonwood trees.

Major Developed Campgrounds	Number of Sites	Water	Showers	Vault Toilets	Flush Toilets	RV Dump Station	Campfire Programs	Picnic Tables/Fire Grates	Boat Ramp	Marina & Supplies	Other
Cimarron	22	X		X	X	X	X	X			
Lake Fork	87	X		X	X	X	X	X	X	X	
Elk Creek	179	X	X	X	X	X	X	X	X	X	
Stevens Creek	54	X			X		X	X	X*		
Campgrounds with Limited Facilities											
East Portal	15	X			X			X			
Ponderosa	21	X			X			X	X		horse corral
Gateview	7	X			X			X			
Red Creek	7	X			X			X			
Dry Gulch	10	X			X			X			
East Elk Creek (Group)	2**	X			X			X			picnic tables
Boat-In & Hike-In	8										

* Small boats only.
** Accommodates total of 50 people; reservations required.

Great Sand Dunes National Monument

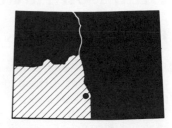

For Information

Great Sand Dunes National Monument
Mosca, CO 81146
(719) 378-2312

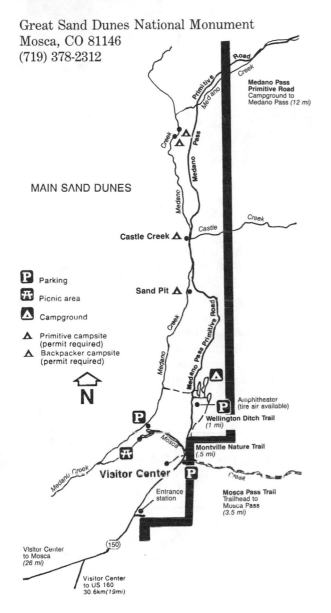

MAIN SAND DUNES

Medano Pass
Primitive Road
Campground to
Medano Pass (12 mi)

Castle Creek ▲

P Parking

🏕 Picnic area

🔺 Campground

▲ Primitive campsite
(permit required)

▲ Backpacker campsite
(permit required)

Sand Pit ▲

N

Amphitheater
(tire air available)

Wellington Ditch Trail
(1 mi)

Montville Nature Trail
(.5 mi)

Visitor Center

Entrance
station

Mosca Pass Trail
Trailhead to
Mosca Pass
(3.5 mi)

Visitor Center
to Mosca
(26 mi)

(150)

Visitor Center
to US 160
30.6km(19mi)

Location

Great Sand Dunes National Monument, 61 miles northeast of Alamosa, is reached from US 160 and SH 150 from the south, or from SH 17 and County Rd. Six Mile Lane from the west.

About the Park

North America's tallest sand dunes at this 36,600-acre park were created by southwesterly winds blowing through three low passes of the lofty Sangre de Cristo Mountains that tower 4,000 feet above the valley floor. Trillions of tons of sand have created a dune field covering over 150 square miles. The main dune field of 50 square miles is stable, but the dune surfaces change with each wind. A portion of the Rio Grande National Forest borders the park on the north and east. Elevation of the park at the visitor center is 8,200 feet; designated wilderness area is 33,450 acres.

Spectacular dune views can be had regardless of age or handicap. Hiking on the dunes is most pleasant early and late in the day. Surface temperatures in the summer can reach 140°F at midday. There are no trails on the dunes; most visitors begin their walk on the dunes from the picnic area. A walk to the top and back requires about 3 hours. The campground and picnic area are among cottonwood trees. The *Pinon Flats Campground* is open April through October with complete facilities; November through March with no facilities. The park is open 24 hours a day year-round; Visitor Center is closed on federal holidays.

Facilities & Activities

88 campsites (no reservations)
3 sites for organized groups (tents only; reservations required: 1 site for 25 max. 2 sites for 50 max.)
modern restrooms
backcountry camping (free permit required)
trailer dump station
picnic area
visitor center/exhibits
nature walks
dune climbing
hiking trails
4-wheel drive auto tours along Medano Primitive Road (concessioner trips, May through September)
amphitheater
ranger hikes, walks, talks and campfire programs with rangers (Memorial Day to Labor Day)
cross-country skiing and snowshoeing, with adequate snowfall
groceries, gasoline, private campground with hookups, etc. located 4 miles south of entrance

Gunnison National Forest

For Information

Grand Mesa-Uncompahgre and Gunnison
 National Forests Headquarters
2250 Highway 50
Delta, CO 81416
(303) 874-7691

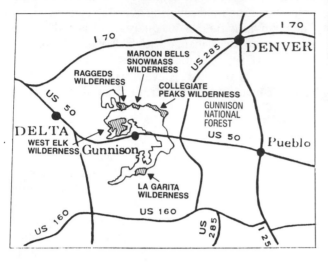

*Hang in there . . . you've
come a long way!*

Location

Gunnison National Forest, one of the largest in Colorado, is in the heart of the Rockies. The 1,663,000-acre forest contains 27 peaks more than 12,000 feet high, buttes, lakes, reservoirs, ghost towns, and geologic formations in West Elk Wilderness Area. The West Elk and portions of the Collegiate Peaks, LaGarita, Maroon Bells-Snowmass, and Raggeds wildernesses cover 367,000 acres of the Gunnison National Forest. The Gunnison, Grand Mesa, and Uncompahgre national forests were administratively combined in 1976.

Wilderness Areas

Collegiate Peaks Wilderness covers 159,900 acres on three national forests: Gunnison, White River, and San Isabel. The area contains 8 peaks over 14,000 feet high. Climbers should consult reliable guidebooks and seek advice from knowledgeable climbers who are familiar with these peaks. Timberline lakes and high mountain streams offer excellent fishing and scenery.

La Garita Wilderness encompasses 103,986 acres on the Gunnison and Rio Grande national forests. "La Garita" means "The Overlook." Ele-

vations within the wilderness range from 9,000 to over 14,000 feet. Over 100 miles of constructed trails are available. Some points of interest in the La Garita Wilderness are San Louis Peak (14,014 feet high), Machin Lake, Mineral Creek, Organ Mountain, Stewart Peak, Baldy Cinco, and Baldy Alto. The Continental Divide National Scenic Trail runs through the area and along its southern boundary.

Maroon Bells-Snowmass Wilderness encompasses more than 174,000 acres on the White River and Gunnison National Forests. Elevations within the wilderness range from 9,000 to over 14,000 feet. Over 100 miles of constructed trails are available for both foot and horse travel through sometimes rugged terrain.

Raggeds Wilderness encompasses more than 59,000 acres on the White River and Gunnison national forests. Elevations within the wilderness range from 7,000 to over 13,000 feet. Over 90 miles of constructed trails are available. Weather for the area can vary greatly; but generally, you can expect cool mountain climate with scattered rain showers throughout the summer months. Normally, the Raggeds Wilderness area is snow-free from July to September, but conditions depend on the elevation and amount of snowfall each winter.

West Elk Wilderness encompasses more than 176,000 acres on the Gunnison National Forest. Elevations within the wilderness range from 7,000 to over 13,000 feet. Over 200 miles of constructed trails are available. Some points of interest in the West Elk are the Castles, West Elk Peak, Sheep Lake, North/Middle/South Baldy Mountain, West and East Beckwith Mountain.

Cebolla Ranger District

For Information

Cebolla Ranger District
216 North Colorado
Gunnison, CO 81230
(303) 641-0471

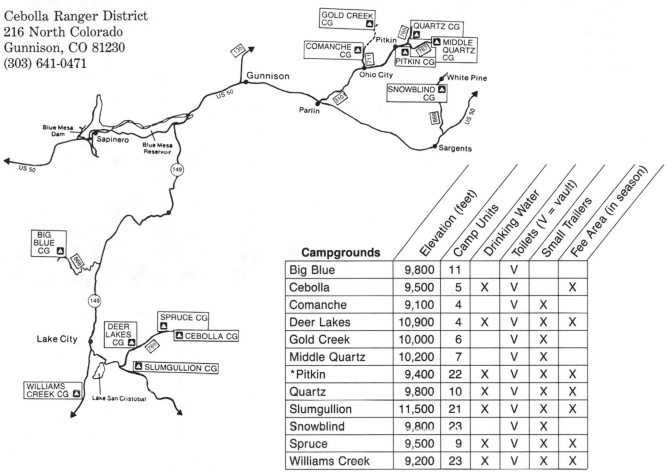

Campgrounds	Elevation (feet)	Camp Units	Drinking Water	Toilets (V = vault)	Small Trailers	Fee Area (in season)
Big Blue	9,800	11		V		
Cebolla	9,500	5	X	V		X
Comanche	9,100	4		V	X	
Deer Lakes	10,900	4	X	V	X	X
Gold Creek	10,000	6		V	X	
Middle Quartz	10,200	7		V	X	
*Pitkin	9,400	22	X	V	X	X
Quartz	9,800	10	X	V	X	X
Slumgullion	11,500	21	X	V	X	X
Snowblind	9,800	23		V	X	
Spruce	9,500	9	X	V	X	X
Williams Creek	9,200	23	X	V	X	X

* On MISTIX reservation system.

Campground Locations

Comanche, Gold Creek, Pitkin, Middle Quartz, Quartz and Snowblind campgrounds are all located in the Pitkin area. Parlin is southeast of Gunnison on US 50; Ohio City is 12 miles northeast of Parlin on BLM Route 3101; Pitkin is 8 miles beyond Ohio City:

—Comanche is 2 miles northeast of Ohio City on Forest Road 771.

—Gold Creek is 7 miles northeast of Ohio City on Forest Road 771.

—Pitkin is 1 mile east of Pitkin on Forest Road 765.

—Middle Quartz is 1½ miles east of Pitkin on Forest Road 765; then 5½ miles east on Forest Road 767.

—Quartz is 4 miles north of Pitkin on Forest Road 765.

—Snowblind is off of US 50 beyond Sargents; travel 1½ miles northeast of Sargents, then 7 miles north on Forest Road 888.

Cebolla, Spruce, Deer Lakes, Slumgullion, Williams Creek, and Big Blue are all located in the Lake City Area. Lake City is southwest of Gunnison on SH 149:

—Big Blue is reached by traveling 11 miles north of Lake City, then approximately 8 miles west on Forest Road 868.

—Williams Creek is reached by traveling 2 miles south of Lake City on SH 149, then right on BLM Route 3306 for 6 miles.

—4 campgrounds are located on Forest Road 788; go 9 miles southeast of Lake City on SH 149 and turn left. From this cut-off, Slumgullion is ¹⁄₁₀ mile, Deer Lakes is 3½ miles, Spruce is 8 miles and Cebolla is 8.8 miles.

Paonia Ranger District

For Information

Paonia Ranger District
North Rio Grande Avenue
P.O. Box 1030
Paonia, CO 81428
(303) 527-4131

Campgrounds	Elevation (feet)	Camp Units	Drinking Water	Toilets (V = vault)	Small Trailers	Fee Area (in season)
Erikson Springs	6,700	18	X	V	X	X
Lost Lake	9,600	11		V	X	
McClure	9,100	19	X	V	X	X

Paonia Reservoir, the site of Paonia State Recreation Area, is surrounded by the Gunnison National Forest.

Campground Locations

Erikson Springs—off of SH 133 that runs from Hotchkiss (east of Delta) to Glenwood Springs. Approximately 6½ miles east of Somerset, just before Paonia Reservoir, turn right on County Road 12 and travel 6 miles to the campground.

Lost Lake—may be reached by going past Erikson Springs Campground on County Road 12 another 8 miles, then south for 3 miles on Forest Road 706. Or it may be reached from Crested Butte, 15 miles to the east.

McClure—on SH 133 north of Paonia Reservoir and 8½ miles southwest of Redstone.

Taylor River Ranger District

For Information

Taylor Ranger District
216 North Colorado
Gunnison, CO 81230
(303) 641-0471

Campground Locations

Soap Creek and *Commissary*—both located north of Blue Mesa Dam off of SH 92. From Gunnison, go 26 miles west on US 50, then 6/10 mile north-west on SH 92 to forest road 721. Soap Creek is 7 miles north, then 6/10 mile northeast on Forest Road 824. Commissary is 2 miles farther north on Forest Road 721.

Almont—north of Gunnison on SH 135, just 1 mile before you reach Almont.

Cement Creek—southeast of Crested Butte; take SH 135 southeast for 7½ miles, then 4 miles northeast on Forest Road 740.

Lake Irwin—7 miles west of Crested Butte on County Road 12; then 2½ miles north on Forest Road 826.

Taylor River Ranger District (continued)

Avery Peak and *Gothic*—both located on Forest Road 317 north of Crested Butte; go north through Mt. Crested Butte, then approximately 5 miles north on Forest Road 317 to Avery Peak. Gothic is ½ mile beyond Avery Peak.

Taylor Canyon Campground—located 7 miles northeast of Almont on Forest Road 742 and *Lakeview Campground* (on the south end of Taylor Park Reservoir) is 23 miles from Almont on this same forest road. Six other campgrounds are located along this canyon road be-

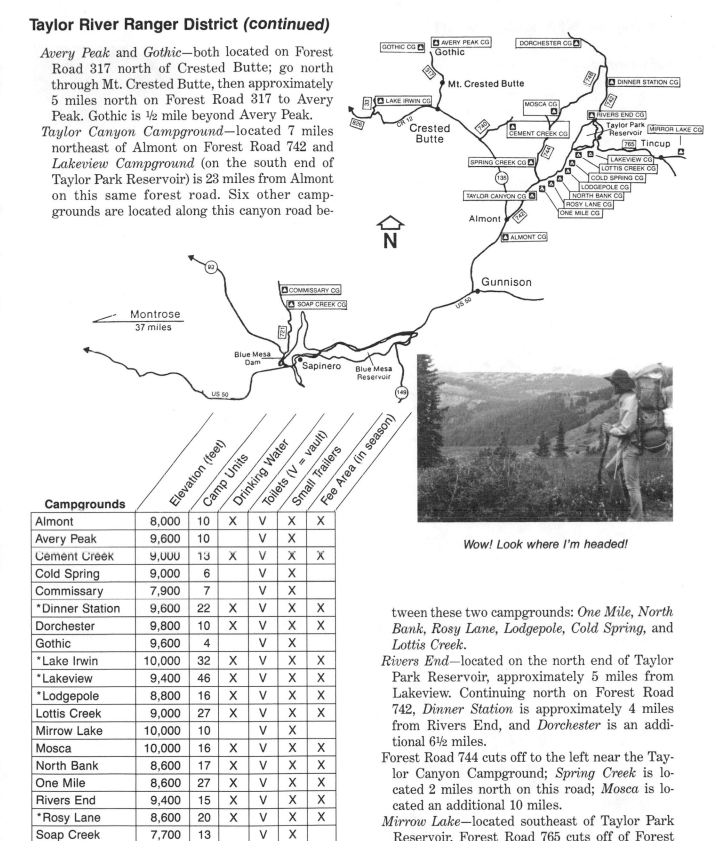

Wow! Look where I'm headed!

Campgrounds	Elevation (feet)	Camp Units	Drinking Water	Toilets (V = vault)	Small Trailers	Fee Area (in season)
Almont	8,000	10	X	V	X	X
Avery Peak	9,600	10		V	X	
Cement Creek	9,000	13	X	V	X	X
Cold Spring	9,000	6		V	X	
Commissary	7,900	7		V	X	
*Dinner Station	9,600	22	X	V	X	X
Dorchester	9,800	10	X	V	X	X
Gothic	9,600	4		V	X	
*Lake Irwin	10,000	32	X	V	X	X
*Lakeview	9,400	46	X	V	X	X
*Lodgepole	8,800	16	X	V	X	X
Lottis Creek	9,000	27	X	V	X	X
Mirrow Lake	10,000	10		V	X	
Mosca	10,000	16	X	V	X	X
North Bank	8,600	17	X	V	X	X
One Mile	8,600	27	X	V	X	X
Rivers End	9,400	15	X	V	X	X
*Rosy Lane	8,600	20	X	V	X	X
Soap Creek	7,700	13		V	X	
Spring Creek	8,600	12	X	V	X	X
Taylor Canyon	8,600	5		V		

* On MISTIX reservation system.

tween these two campgrounds: *One Mile, North Bank, Rosy Lane, Lodgepole, Cold Spring*, and *Lottis Creek*.

Rivers End—located on the north end of Taylor Park Reservoir, approximately 5 miles from Lakeview. Continuing north on Forest Road 742, *Dinner Station* is approximately 4 miles from Rivers End, and *Dorchester* is an additional 6½ miles.

Forest Road 744 cuts off to the left near the Taylor Canyon Campground; *Spring Creek* is located 2 miles north on this road; *Mosca* is located an additional 10 miles.

Mirrow Lake—located southeast of Taylor Park Reservoir. Forest Road 765 cuts off of Forest Road 742 as it circles the south side of the reservoir; take this road southeast for 7½ miles to Tincup, then 3 miles east on Forest Road 267.

REGION 3

Gunnison National Forest 127

Mancos State Recreation Area

For Information

Mancos State Recreation Area
c/o Navajo State Recreation Area
Box 1697
Arboles, CO 81121
(303) 883-2208

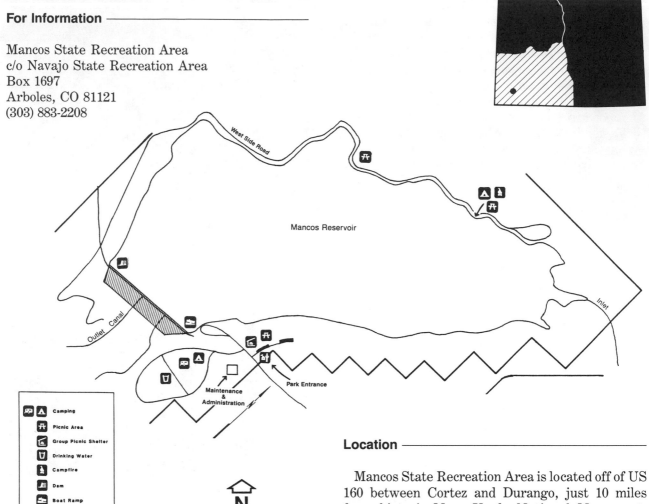

Legend

- 🏕 🏕 Camping
- 🛖 Picnic Area
- 🏠 Group Picnic Shelter
- 🚰 Drinking Water
- 🔥 Campfire
- ⛩ Dam
- 🚤 Boat Ramp

N

Beautiful trees line the banks of the Mancos Reservoir.

Location

Mancos State Recreation Area is located off of US 160 between Cortez and Durango, just 10 miles from historic Mesa Verde National Monument. From Mancos, go north on SH 184 about ¼ mile and turn east onto County Rd. 42 (FSR 561). Go 4 miles and take County Rd. N to the park entrance. The reservoir has 215 surface acres for recreation; the total of land acres is 338. This area is surrounded by beautiful mountain scenery and has a pleasant climate at an elevation of 7,800 feet.

Facilities & Activities

33 campsites
picnic sites
covered group shelter
boating (wakeless)
boat ramp
fishing
sailboarding
snowmobiling
cross-country skiing
ice fishing
4 miles of hiking/horseback trails

Mesa Verde National Park

For Information

Mesa Verde National Park
Mesa Verde, CO 81330
(303) 529-4461

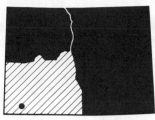

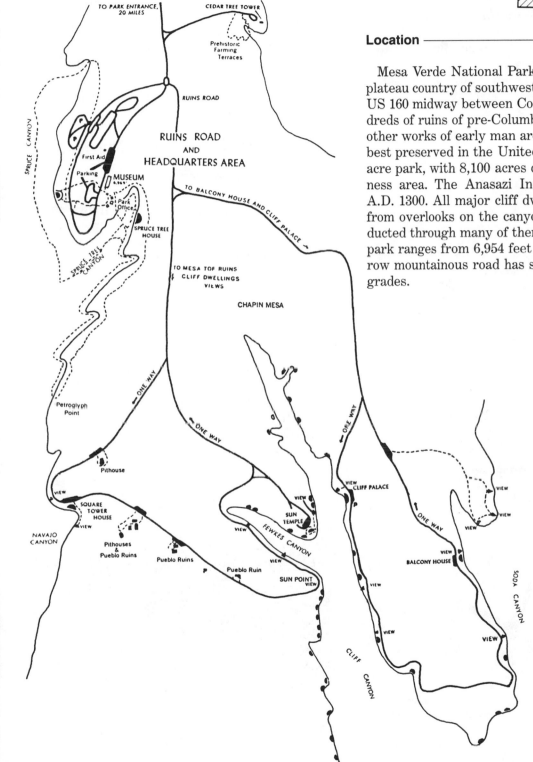

Location

Mesa Verde National Park is located in the high plateau country of southwestern Colorado, south of US 160 midway between Cortez and Mancos. Hundreds of ruins of pre-Columbian cliff dwellings and other works of early man are the most notable and best preserved in the United States at this 52,085-acre park, with 8,100 acres designated as a wilderness area. The Anasazi Indians lived here until A.D. 1300. All major cliff dwellings can be viewed from overlooks on the canyon rims; tours are conducted through many of them. The elevation of the park ranges from 6,954 feet to 8,572 feet. The narrow mountainous road has sharp curves and steep grades.

REGION 3

Mesa Verde National Park (continued)

Facilities & Activities at Morefield Campground

Morefield Campground is located 4 miles south of the park entrance

Campground is open from May 1 through October; exact dates depend on road and snow conditions

first-come, first-served; no reservations are taken

477 campsites with picnic table and fireplace with grill, including 15 with full hookups

6 campsites accessible to physically impaired persons

trailer dump stations

modern restrooms

17 group camping sites; 25-person maximum (reservations required: phone 303/533-7731)

picnic facilities

1,600-seat outdoor amphitheater

nightly ranger programs (mid-June through Labor Day)

non-denominational religious services in summer

trailhead for 3 hiking trails

   Prater Ridge (7.8 miles; approximately 3 hours)

   Point Lookout (2.3 miles; approximately 1½ hours)

   Knife Edge (1.5 miles; approximately 50 minutes)

campground concessions: gas station, snack bar, store, gift shop, laundry, showers, firewood

for campground information: (303) 529-4474

MOREFIELD CAMPGROUND

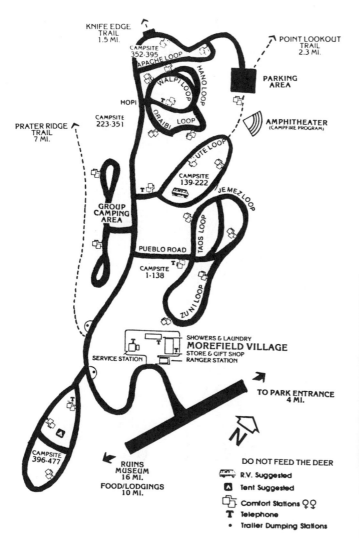

General Park Information

▲ To get the most out of your visit, go first to either the Far View Visitor Center (open only in summer) or to the Chapin Mesa Museum.

▲ The Far View Visitor Center is 15 miles from the park entrance; the Chapin Mesa Museum is 21 miles from the park entrance.

▲ Food, gasoline, and lodging are available only from May through October. No services are available the rest of the year.

▲ Park roads and trails may be hazardous in winter; stop at the entrance gate for current information on road conditions and tour schedules.

▲ Do not tow trailers beyond Morefield Campground.

▲ Bicycling is permitted in the park, but there are no designated lanes.

Cliff Palace is the largest ruin in the park. Its chance discovery in 1888 led to extensive explorations.

Mesa Verde National Park *(continued)*

▲ There is NO backpacking or cross-country hiking in the park.

▲ There is NO overnight backcountry use.

▲ Hiking is allowed only in developed areas on the 5 day-use trails.

▲ Hikers are required to register at the ranger's office for the 2 trails in the Chapin Mesa area: Petroglyph Point Trail (2.8 miles) and Spruce Canyon Trail (2.1 miles).

▲ All trails are closed during winter months.

Mesa Verde National Park is located in the high plateau country; park roads are scenic drives with sharp curves and steep grades.

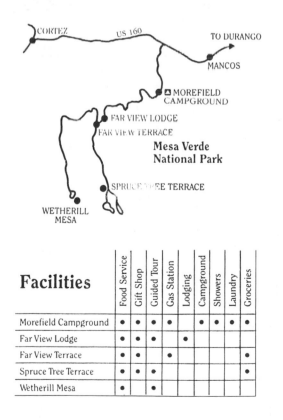

Facilities	Food Service	Gift Shop	Guided Tour	Gas Station	Lodging	Campground	Showers	Laundry	Groceries
Morefield Campground	•	•	•	•		•	•	•	•
Far View Lodge	•	•	•		•				
Far View Terrace	•	•		•					•
Spruce Tree Terrace	•	•	•						•
Wetherill Mesa	•		•						

▲ Picnic facilities are located in the museum area on Chapin Mesa, both loops of the Ruins Road, Morefield Campground and Wetherill Mesa.

▲ Pets must be on a leash; pets are NOT allowed on trails, in ruins, or in buildings.

▲ Self-guiding auto tours are available where mesa-top ruins may be visited and a number of cliff dwellings viewed from canyon rim overlooks.

▲ Cliff dwellings, ruins, pueblo sites, etc. open seasonally for ranger-guided tours and self-guided tours (for specific questions on tours, call the museum at (303) 529-4475.

▲ Most tours are available in the summer only; the Spruce Tree House is the only guided tour available in the winter.

▲ Full interpretive services begin in mid-June & continue through Labor Day.

▲ Archeological museum, interpretive exhibits and talks; wayside exhibits.

▲ Motel accommodations are available at Far View Motor Lodge (early May to mid-October) Summer: (303) 529-4421; Winter: (303) 533-7731.

Three major cliff dwellings on Chapin Mesa are open for visits; many others are visible from Ruins Road.

Navajo State Recreation Area

For Information

Navajo State Recreation Area
Box 1697
Arboles, CO 81121
(303) 883-2208

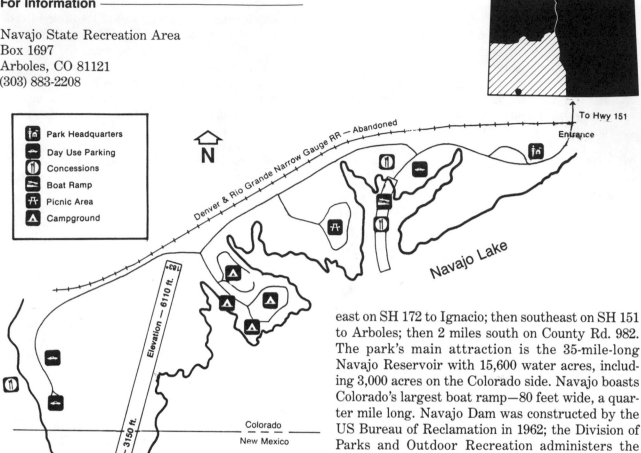

Park Headquarters
Day Use Parking
Concessions
Boat Ramp
Picnic Area
Campground

N

Denver & Rio Grande Narrow Gauge RR — Abandoned

To Hwy 151

Entrance

Navajo Lake

Elevation — 6110 ft.

Length — 3150 ft.

183.

003.

Colorado
New Mexico

Location

Navajo State Recreation Area is located south of US 160 between Durango and Pagosa Springs on the Colorado-New Mexico border. From Pagosa Springs, take US 160 west for 17 miles; turn southwest on SH 151, go 18 miles to the town of Arboles; then 2 miles south on County Rd. 982. From Durango, take US 160 east for 8 miles; travel south-

east on SH 172 to Ignacio; then southeast on SH 151 to Arboles; then 2 miles south on County Rd. 982. The park's main attraction is the 35-mile-long Navajo Reservoir with 15,600 water acres, including 3,000 acres on the Colorado side. Navajo boasts Colorado's largest boat ramp—80 feet wide, a quarter mile long. Navajo Dam was constructed by the US Bureau of Reclamation in 1962; the Division of Parks and Outdoor Recreation administers the 2,000-acre Navajo SRA. Elevation: 6,100 feet.

Facilities & Activities

71 campsites
  4 with electrical hookups
showers
dump station
group campground
visitor/nature center
picnic sites
group picnic area available
snackbar
boating
boat ramps
marina
boat rental
fishing
water skiing
sailboarding
winter camping
2½ miles of hiking trails
horseback riding
dirt runway for small aircraft

There is lots of room to jet ski on 35-mile-long Navajo Reservoir.

Colorado Division of Parks and Outdoor Recreation

Paonia State Recreation Area

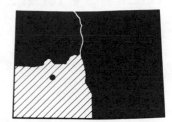

For Information

Paonia State Recreation Area
c/o Crawford State Recreation Area
P.O. Box 147
Crawford, CO 81415
(303) 921-5721

Location

Paonia State Recreation Area, located south of Glenwood Springs, has been described as a Scandinavian fjord in Colorado, because the surrounding land above the reservoir is quite steep. Camping is rustic (bring your own drinking water); of the total 1,507 land acres, 1,502 are designated as backcountry. From Glenwood Springs take SH 82 south to Carbondale; then go south on SH 133 over McClure Pass, 46 miles to the 322-acre Paonia Reservoir. Elevation: 6,500 feet.

Facilities & Activities

16 campsites
NO drinking water available
picnic sites
boating
boat ramps
fishing
water skiing

sailboarding
snowmobiling
cross-country skiing
snow tubing
nature trail
horseback riding

Camping is rustic at Paonia . . . you even need to bring your own drinking water.

Water from the 322-acre Paonia Reservoir helps create the North Fork of the Gunnison River.

REGION 3

Ridgway State Recreation Area

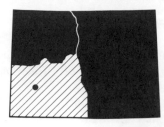

For Information

Ridgway State Recreation Area
28555 Hwy 550
Ridgway, CO 81432
(303) 626-5822

Location

Ridgway State Recreation Area, one of Colorado's newest parks, is located 20 miles south of Montrose and 16 miles north of historic Ouray off of US 550. Ridgway Reservoir is fed by the Uncompahgre River, Alkali Creek, and Dallas Creek. The 2,230-acre park is framed on the south by the majestic San Juan Range and Cimarron Ridge. The 5-mile long and 1-mile-wide reservoir, part of the Colorado River Storage Project, will fluctuate throughout the year. However, the reservoir will be approximately 900–1,000 surface acres from May to August. Ridgway, having the most convenient access of any western slope reservoir, will be developed in 5 stages. Elevation: 6,870 feet.

Ridgway, one of the newest state recreation areas, will be developed in five stages. The Dutch Charlie campground has 200 campsites.

Facilities & Activities

200 campsites
electrical hookups
showers
dump station
laundry
visitor/nature center
picnic sites
swimming
bathhouse
boating
boat ramp
marina
boat rental
fishing
fish cleaning station
water skiing
sailboarding
cross-country skiing
ice fishing
snow tubing
winter camping
5 miles of hiking trails
5 miles of bicycling trails
horseback riding

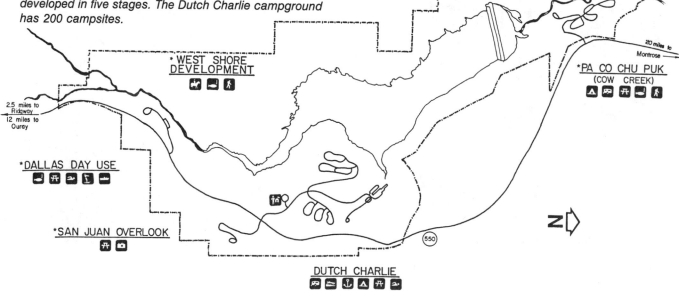

Rio Grande National Forest

For Information

Rio Grande National Forest Headquarters
1803 West Highway 160
Monte Vista, CO 81144
(719) 852-5941

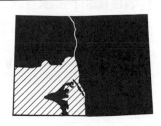

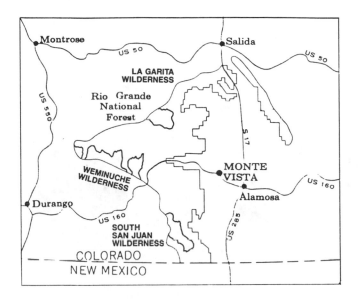

Location

The Rio Grande National Forest includes 1,851,424 acres of publicly owned land on the eastern slope of the Continental Divide. Parts of two spectacular mountain ranges, the San Juan and the Sangre de Cristo, are within the forest. Also included are the headwaters of the third longest river in the United States—the Rio Grande del Norte, or "Great River of the North," as it was known by the early Spanish and Indian inhabitants of the southwest. Between the ranges with their 14,000-foot summits is the fertile San Luis Valley, one of several high "parks" or basins in Colorado, ringed by mountains.

Wilderness Areas

La Garita Wilderness encompasses 103,986 acres on the Gunnison and Rio Grande national forests. "La Garita" means "The Overlook." Elevations within the wilderness range from 9,000 to over 14,000 feet. Over 100 miles of constructed trails are available. Some points of interest in the La Garita Wilderness are San Louis Peak (14,014 feet high), Machin Lake, Mineral Creek, Organ Mountain, Stewart Peak, Baldy Cinco, and Baldy Alto. The Continental Divide National Scenic Trail runs through the area and along its southern boundary.

South San Juan Wilderness contains 216,000 acres with 189,000 acres in the Rio Grande National Forest, and 27,000 acres in the San Juan National Forest. Elevations range from 8,800 to 13,172-foot Conejos Peak. Approximately 260 miles of constructed trails are available for both foot and horse travel through this rugged terrain; numerous lakes exist.

Weminuche Wilderness is one of the nation's newest and largest additions to the wilderness system, having been signed into law by President Ford in 1975. In 1980, the area was expanded to its present 467,400-acre size. The Weminuche is a spectacular region of rugged mountain peaks with an average elevation of 10,000 feet. Three peaks in the area, Mt. Eolus, Sunlight, and Windom, reach more than 14,000 feet and many are over 13,000 feet. Nearly 250 miles of trails traverse the area and many lead to mountain lakes and meadows. The area is named for the Weminuche Indians who used this area for many years.

Wonder if the Weminuche Indians carried loads this heavy when they roamed these trails?

REGION 3

Conejos Peak Ranger District

For Information

Conejos Peak Ranger District
21461 State Highway 285
La Jara, CO 81140
(719) 274-5193

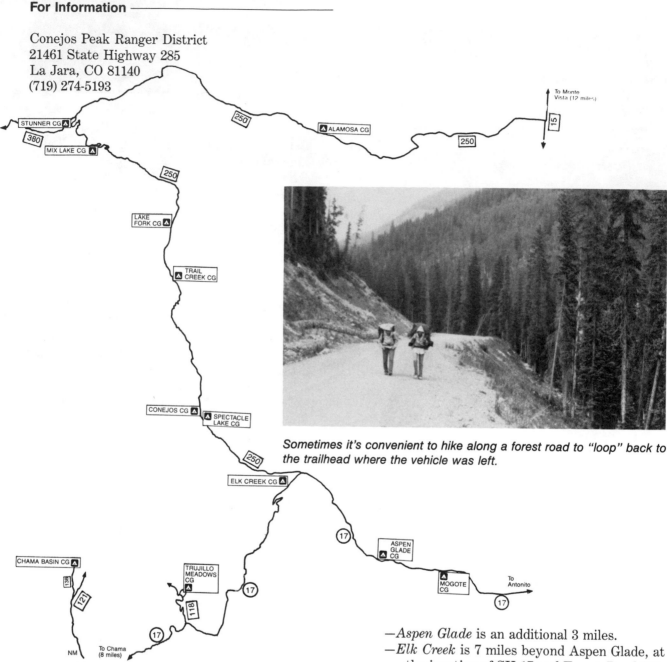

Sometimes it's convenient to hike along a forest road to "loop" back to the trailhead where the vehicle was left.

Campground Locations

Alamosa and *Stunner*—both off of Forest Road 250; from Monte Vista on US 160/285, go 12 miles south on SH 15, then west on Forest Road 250. Alamosa is 17½ miles; Stunner is 34 miles on Forest Road 250, then ¼ mile on Forest Road 380.

10 campgrounds are off of SH 17 west from US 285 at Antonito:

—*Mogote* is 13 miles west on SH 17.

—*Aspen Glade* is an additional 3 miles.

—*Elk Creek* is 7 miles beyond Aspen Glade, at the junction of SH 17 and Forest Road 250.

From this junction of SH 17 and Forest Road 250 (approximately 23 miles from Antonito):

—*Spectacle Lake* is 6 miles on Forest Road 250.

—*Conejos* is 7 miles.

—*Trail Creek* is 13 miles.

—*Lake Fork* is 16 miles.

—*Mix Lake* is 22 miles.

Note: Because Forest Road 250 makes a loop and connects to SH 15 to Monte Vista, these campgrounds could also be approached from that direction.

Conejos Peak Ranger District (continued)

Campgrounds	Elevation (feet)	Camp Units	Drinking Water	Toilets (V = vault)	Small Trailers	Fee Area (in season)
Alamosa	8,600	10	X	V	X	
*Aspen Glade	8,500	34	X	V	X	X
Chama Basin	8,800	15		V	X	
Conejos	9,000	16	X	V	X	X
*Elk Creek	9,600	45	X	V	X	X
Lake Fork	9,600	19	X	V	X	X
Mix Lake	10,100	22	X	V	X	X
*Mogote	8,300	21	X	V	X	X
Spectacle Lake	9,000	24	X	V	X	X
Stunner	9,800	10	X	V	X	
Trail Creek	9,300	20				
Trujillos Meadows	10,400	24	X	V	X	X

* On MISTIX reservation system.
Mogote also has 2 group areas; reservations required.

Trujillo Meadows—located on Trujillo Meadows Reservoir, approximately 35 miles west of Antonito off of SH 17. Turn north on Forest Road 118 before Cumbres Pass and travel 3 miles.

Chama Basin—off of SH 17 between Chama, NM and Antonito and is reached by traveling into New Mexico, then north on Forest Road 121, then Forest Road 738 for approximately 2 miles.

Even a bridge this dilapidated can be a welcome sight when looking for a way to cross a stream.

Creede Ranger District

For Information

Creede Ranger District
3rd and Creede Avenue
P.O. Box 270
Creede, CO 81130
(719) 658-2556

Campground Locations

Palisade is located 12 miles southeast of Creede on SH 149 adjacent to the Rio Grande River.

Five campgrounds are located west from Creede on SH 149 or immediately off of SH 149:
—*Marshall Park* is 6 miles from Creede.
—*Rio Grande Campground* is 8½ miles to the intersection of a dirt road to the south (sign on right reads "Rio Grande Fisherman Area"), then approximately 1 mile on dirt road.
—*South Clear Creek* is 22½ miles from Creede, then ¼ mile north on Forest Road 510.

—*North Clear Creek* can also be reached via Forest Road 510 by traveling approximately 2 miles.
—*South Clear Creek Falls* is 23.7 miles from Creede off of SH 149.

Ivy Creek Campground is located 16 miles southwest of Creede on Forest Road 526. Travel southwest on SH 149 for 6 miles, turn left on Forest Road 523 (Middle Creek Road) and go south for approximately 4 miles, then left on Forest Road 528 (Lime Creek Road) for 3 miles, then right on Forest Road 526 (Red Mountain Road) for 3 miles to the campground.

Four campgrounds are located on Forest Road #520 (Rio Grande Reservoir Road); this road cuts off of SH 149 just 20 miles west from Creede:
—*River Hill* is 9½ miles from the SH 149/FR 520 intersection.
—*Road Canyon* is 6 miles.
—*Thirty-Mile* is 11 miles.
—*Lost Trail* is 18 miles.

Creede Ranger District *(continued)*

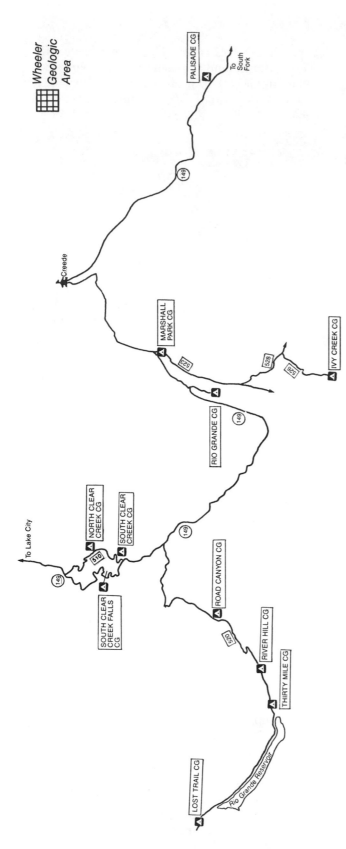

Wheeler Geologic Area

Wheeler Geologic Area is located about a mile and a half south of the Continental Divide. Contact the Creede Ranger District for trail maps and other information about this scenic area.

Campgrounds	Elevation (feet)	Camp Units	Drinking Water	Toilets (V = vault)	Small Trailers	Fee Area (in season)
Ivy Creek	9,200	4		V		
Lost Trail	9,500	7	X	V		
*Marshall Park	8,800	15	X	V	X	X
North Clear Creek	9,800	25	X	V	X	X
*Palisade	8,300	13	X	V	X	X
Rio Grande	8,900	4	X	V	X	
River Hill	9,300	20	X	F	X	X
Road Canyon	9,300	5	X	V	X	
South Clear Creek	9,500	16	X	V	X	X
South Clear Creek Falls	9,700	11	X	V	X	X
Thirty-Mile	9,300	35	X	F	X	X

* On MISTIX reservation system.

Del Norte Ranger District

For Information

Del Norte Ranger District
13308 West Highway 160
P.O. Box 40
Del Norte, CO 81132
(719) 657-3321

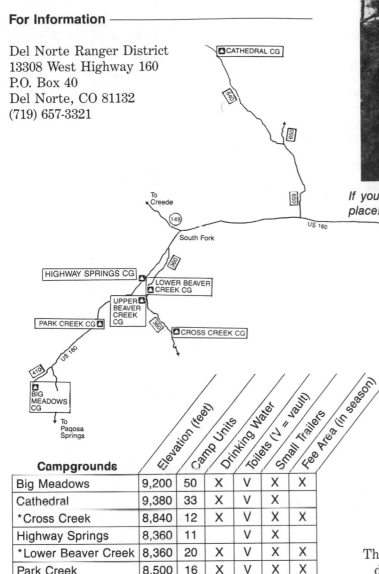

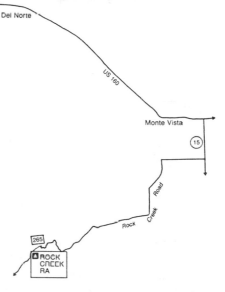

If you're looking for solitude, this could be the perfect place!

Campgrounds	Elevation (feet)	Camp Units	Drinking Water	Toilets (V = vault)	Small Trailers	Fee Area (in season)
Big Meadows	9,200	50	X	V	X	X
Cathedral	9,380	33	X	V	X	
*Cross Creek	8,840	12	X	V	X	X
Highway Springs	8,360	11		V	X	
*Lower Beaver Creek	8,360	20	X	V	X	X
Park Creek	8,500	16	X	V	X	X
Rock Creek	9,400	13		V	X	
Upper Beaver Creek	8,400	15	X	V	X	X

* On MISTIX reservation system.

Campground Locations

Highway Springs is 4 miles southwest of South Fork on US 160 on the south side of the highway.

Park Creek is 6½ miles southwest of South Fork on US 160 on the south side of the highway; the campground entrance is ¼ mile west of the Park Creek Forest Road intersection.

Big Meadows is 12½ miles southwest of South Fork on US 160, then 1½ miles west on Forest Road 410.

Three campgrounds are in the Beaver Creek drainage southwest of South Fork. Take US 160 southwest for 1 mile to Forest Road 360 and turn left:
—*Lower Beaver Creek* is 4½ miles.
—*Upper Beaver Creek* is 5 miles.
—*Cross Creek* is 9 miles south, past Beaver Creek Reservoir.

Rock Creek is 16 miles southwest of SH 15 out of Monte Vista. Take SH 15 south for 2 miles, then Rock Creek Road for 12 miles southwest to the forest boundary where it becomes Forest Road 265. The campground is less than 2 miles within the forest.

Cathedral is northwest of Del Norte on Embargo Creek. From the Del Norte Ranger Station go 8¾ miles west on US 160. Take the Embargo Creek Forest Road (#650 & later #640) north for 12 miles to the campground.

REGION 3

Saguache Ranger District

For Information

Saguache Ranger District
626 Gunnison Ave.
P.O. Box 67
Saguache, CO 81149
(719) 655-2553

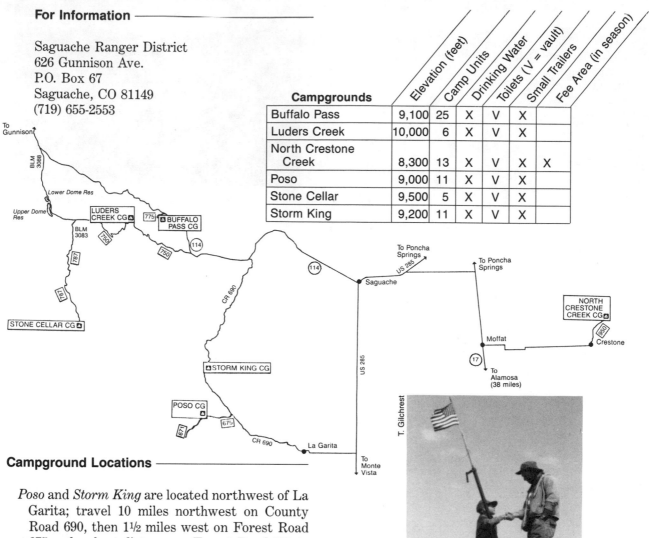

Campgrounds	Elevation (feet)	Camp Units	Drinking Water	Toilets (V = vault)	Small Trailers	Fee Area (in season)
Buffalo Pass	9,100	25	X	V	X	
Luders Creek	10,000	6	X	V	X	
North Crestone Creek	8,300	13	X	V	X	X
Poso	9,000	11	X	V	X	
Stone Cellar	9,500	5	X	V	X	
Storm King	9,200	11	X	V	X	

Campground Locations

Poso and *Storm King* are located northwest of La Garita; travel 10 miles northwest on County Road 690, then 1½ miles west on Forest Road 675 and a short distance on Forest Road 671 to reach Poso. Where County Road 690 enters the forest, continue for 4½ miles on Forest Road 690 to Storm King. Note: La Garita is reached by traveling 19 miles north of Monte Vista on US 285, then 6 miles west.

North Crestone Creek is located approximately 2½ miles north of Crestone on Forest Road 950. Note: Crestone is reached by traveling 38 miles north of Alamosa on SH 17 to Moffat, then 12 miles east to Crestone.

Luders Creek is northwest of Saguache; travel 22 miles on SH 114, then 11 miles northwest on Forest Road 750.

Buffalo Pass is 27½ miles northwest of Saguache on SH 114; take Forest Road 775 to the left for 1½ miles.

The route to *Stone Cellar*, a small undeveloped campground, is more easily found with the aid of a national forest map. In fact, the Gunnison

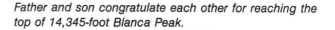

Father and son congratulate each other for reaching the top of 14,345-foot Blanca Peak.

National Forest map shows all of the roads more clearly than does the Rio Grande National Forest map. Traveling from Gunnison on SH 114, take the road that goes to Lower and Upper Dome Reservoir (BLM Route 3083). About 2 miles past Upper Dome Reservoir, turn right on BLM Route 3088. This road becomes Forest Road 787 after approximately 2 miles; continue on for approximately 10 more miles to the campground.

San Isabel National Forest

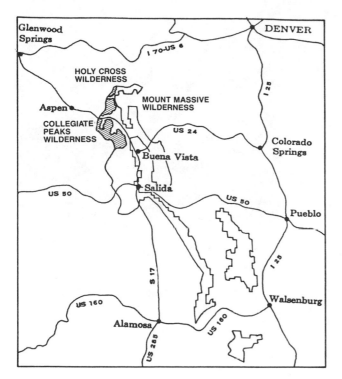

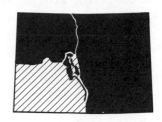

For Information

Pike and San Isabel National
    Forest Headquarters
1920 Valley Drive
Pueblo, CO 81008
(719) 545-8737

Location

San Isabel National Forest encompasses 1,237,920 acres and has the highest average elevation of any national forest. Elevations range from 6,000 feet to the highest peak in Colorado, the 14,433-foot Mt. Elbert, one of 17 mountain peaks 14,000 feet and over in this forest.

Special Notes

The high mountain peaks of the Sangre de Cristo Range, the Spanish Peaks, the Collegiate Peaks, and the Sawatch Range offer some outstanding scenic beauty. For the expert and novice climber, these mountains offer some challenging and rewarding effort. The 14,421-foot Mt. Massive is the second highest peak in Colorado. Both Mt. Massive and Mt. Elbert can be climbed by those with no mountain climbing experience. Trails lead to the summits of both peaks; one full day should be allowed for ascent and return.

The Spanish Peaks, near La Veta, are important landmarks of the Southwest. Their isolated location and abrupt rise of 7,000 feet above the Great Plains made them of special significance to Indian tribes, Spanish explorers, and American frontiersmen. The Great Dikes are among the unusual geologic features of the Spanish Peaks; they radiate out from the mountains like spokes of a wheel. These walls are spectacular in height and length. A scenic drive around the peaks offers outstanding photographic opportunities.

Wilderness Areas

Collegiate Peaks Wilderness covers 159,900 acres on three national forests: Gunnison, White River, and San Isabel. The area contains eight peaks over 14,000 feet high. Climbers should consult reliable guidebooks and seek advice from knowledgeable climbers who are familiar with these peaks. Timberline lakes and high mountain streams offer excellent fishing and scenery.

Holy Cross Wilderness, located about 10 miles northwest of Leadville, on the San Isabel and the White River national forests lies astride the Continental Divide. It was named for the widely known 14,005-foot Mount of the Holy Cross. The wilderness contains numerous high peaks along with scenic basins and valleys dotted with small natural lakes near timberline.

Mount Massive Wilderness near Leadville, along the Continental Divide, is dominated by and includes Colorado's second highest peak, Mt. Massive at 14,421 feet elevation. The wilderness joins the White River National Forest's Hunter Fryingpan Wilderness along the Continental Divide. The area is characterized by alpine mountains and ridges sloping off the spruce-fir and lodgepole pine forests at lower elevations. High mountain lakes are numerous.

Leadville Ranger District

For Information

Leadville Ranger District
2015 North Poplar
Leadville, CO 80461
(719) 486-0752

Campgrounds	Elevation (feet)	Camp Units	Drinking Water	Toilets (V = vault)	Small Trailers	Fee Area (in season)
*Baby Doe	9,900	50	X	V	X	X
[1] Belle of Colorado	9,900	19	X	V		X
[2] Dexter	9,500	26	X	V	X	X
Elbert Creek	10,100	17	X	V	X	X
*Father Dyer	9,900	26	X	V	X	X
Halfmoon	9,900	24	X	V	X	X
Lakeview	9,500	59	X	V	X	X
May Queen	9,900	34	X	V	X	X
*Molly Brown	9,900	49	X	V	X	X
Parry Peak	9,500	26	X	V	X	X
*Silver Dollar	9,900	45	X	V	X	X
[2] *Tabor	9,900	20	X	V	X	X
Twin Peaks	9,600	37	X	V	X	X
White Star	9,500	64	X	V	X	X
**Printerboy	9,900		X	V	X	X

* On MISTIX reservation system.
** Group campground; reservations required.
[1] Tents only; [2] self-contained only.

Campground Locations

Halfmoon and *Elbert Creek* are both located southwest of Leadville. For Halfmoon, travel 3.7 miles west of Leadville on US 24, then ¾ mile west on SH 300; then 5½ miles southwest on Forest Road 110. Elbert Creek is 1 mile beyond Halfmoon.

Hiking in the rain can be refreshing or depressing, but be careful of slippery trails in either case.

A group of climbers are enjoying their lunch break in the high country.

N. L. Gilchrest

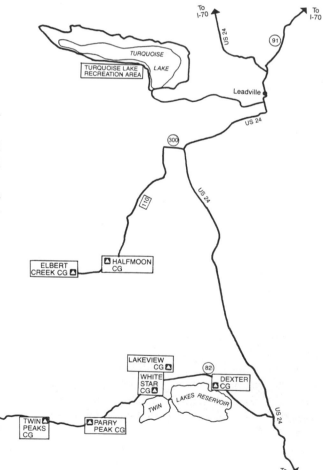

Leadville Ranger District *(continued)*

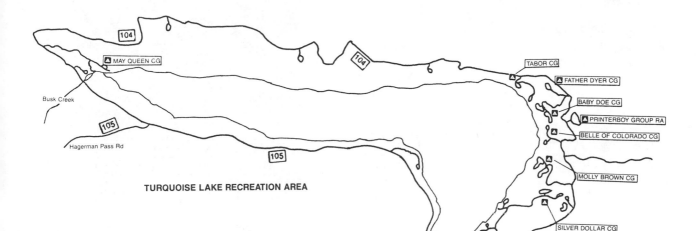

TURQUOISE LAKE RECREATION AREA

Turquoise Lake Recreation Area, 6 miles west of Leadville, has 8 campgrounds. From Leadville, take Forest Road 105 west to Forest Road 104, turn right and head north to encircle the lake counterclockwise. *Silver Dollar Campground* is the first campground; then, in order are *Molly Brown, Belle of Colorado, Printerboy Group Camp, Baby Doe, Father Dyer, Tabor,* and at the west end of the lake is *May Queen.*

Twin Lakes Recreation Area is south of Leadville, on SH 82 to Aspen from US 24. The area has 5 campgrounds. *Dexter, Lakeview,* and *White Star* are located on the north side of the lake off of SH 82; *Parry Peaks* and *Twin Peaks* are located west of Twin Lakes.

Mt. Elbert is Colorado's highest peak. Located southwest of Leadville, the mountain reaches an elevation of 14,433 feet above sea level.

Would you believe that the pile of rocks on which father and son stand is that same mountain?

REGION 3

Salida Ranger District

For Information

Salida Ranger District
230 West 16th
Salida, CO 81201
(719) 539-3591

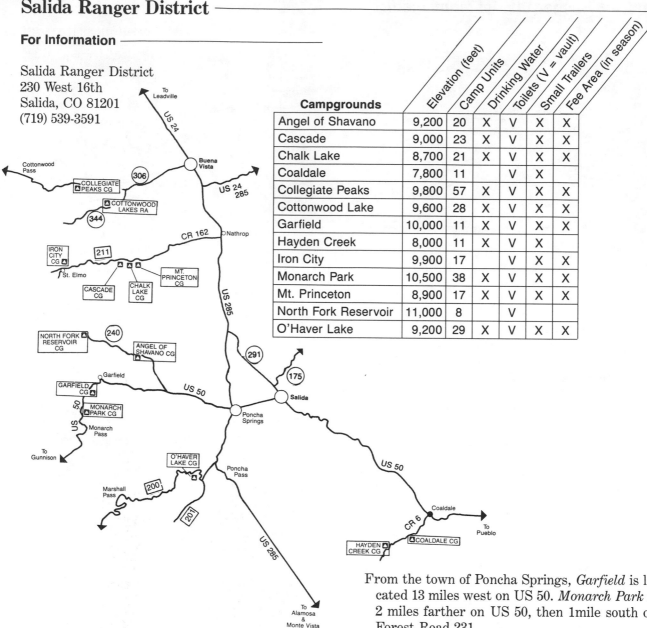

Campgrounds	Elevation (feet)	Camp Units	Drinking Water	Toilets (V = vault)	Small Trailers	Fee Area (in season)
Angel of Shavano	9,200	20	X	V	X	X
Cascade	9,000	23	X	V	X	X
Chalk Lake	8,700	21	X	V	X	X
Coaldale	7,800	11		V	X	
Collegiate Peaks	9,800	57	X	V	X	X
Cottonwood Lake	9,600	28	X	V	X	X
Garfield	10,000	11	X	V	X	X
Hayden Creek	8,000	11	X	V	X	
Iron City	9,900	17		V	X	X
Monarch Park	10,500	38	X	V	X	X
Mt. Princeton	8,900	17	X	V	X	X
North Fork Reservoir	11,000	8		V		
O'Haver Lake	9,200	29	X	V	X	X

Campground Locations

Cottonwood Lake and *Collegiate Peaks* are both located west of US 24 at Buena Vista on County Road 306. When the road forks at approximately 7 miles, go right on Forest Road 306 for 4 miles to Collegiate Peaks, or go left on Forest Road 344 for 4 miles to Cottonwood Lake.

Four campgrounds are located west of US 285 at Nathrop on County Road 162/Forest Road 211:
—*Iron City* is 15 miles from Nathrop.
—*Cascade* is 9 miles.
—*Chalk Lake* is 8 miles.
—*Mt. Princeton* is 7 miles.

From the town of Poncha Springs, *Garfield* is located 13 miles west on US 50. *Monarch Park* is 2 miles farther on US 50, then 1mile south on Forest Road 231.

To reach *North Fork Reservoir* and *Angel of Shavano*, travel 6 miles west on US 50: then north for 4 miles on Forest Road 240 for *Angel of Shavano* and an additional 6 miles for *North Fork Reservoir.*

O'Haver Lake is southwest of Poncha Springs. Travel 5 miles south on US 285, then west on County Road 200 for 2.3 miles, then west on County Road 202 for 1½ miles.

Hayden Creek and *Coaldale* are both located southwest of Salida. By way of US 50 go 18 miles to the little town of Coaldale; then 4 miles southwest on County Road 6 (becomes Forest Road 249) for *Hayden Creek* and just 3 miles for *Coaldale Campground.*

San Juan National Forest

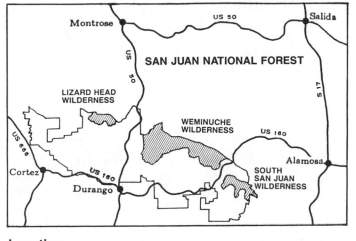

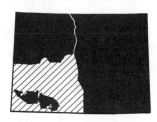

Location

The San Juan National Forest, located in southwestern Colorado encompasses over two million acres. Elevations range from over 14,000 feet on the higher peaks to less than 8,000 feet in the foothills. Snowfall at the higher elevations is very heavy from late October until April, and does not leave the high passes and basins until mid-summer. Some points of interest in the forest include Treasure Falls, Chimney Rock, Dolores River Canyon, La Plata Canyon, Vallecito Reservoir, Needle Mountains and Emerald Lake.

Wilderness Areas

Lizard Head Wilderness, north of Rico, encompasses 40,000 acres. This wilderness area is popular with climbers. Within the area, the San Miguel Mountains consist of two distinct clusters of peaks. The eastern cluster, informally called the Wilson Group, contains Mount Wilson (14,246 feet), El Diente Peak (14,159 feet), Wilson Peak (14,017 feet) and South Wilson (14,110 feet). Two miles east is the spectacular landmark of Lizard Head, a nearly vertical rock spire that rises 300 feet from a conical base to 13,113 feet. A saddle two miles in length separates the eastern cluster from the western cluster of peaks called the Dolores Peak Group, a smaller cluster of three peaks that reach a maximum elevation of 13,290 feet at Dolores Peak.

South San Juan Wilderness contains 216,000, with 189,000 acres in the Rio Grande National Forest, and 27,000 acres in the San Juan National Forest. Elevations range from 8,800 to 13,172-foot Conejos Peak. Approximately 260 miles of constructed trails are available for both foot and horse travel through this rugged terrain; numerous lakes exist.

Weminuche Wilderness is one of the nation's newest and largest additions to the wilderness system, having been signed into law by President Ford in 1975. In 1980, the area was expanded to its present 467,400-acre size. The Weminuche is a spectacular region of rugged mountain peaks with an average elevation of 10,000 feet. Three peaks in the area, Mts. Eolus, Sunlight, and Windom, reach more than 14,000 feet and many are over 13,000 feet. Nearly 250 miles of trails traverse the area and many lead to mountain lakes and meadows. The area is named for the Weminuche Indians who used this area for many years.

For Information

San Juan National Forest Headquarters
701 Camino del Rio, Room 301
Durango, CO 81301
(303) 247-4874

Backpackers begin their descent into Chicago Basin. Destination: the suspension bridge across the Animas River.

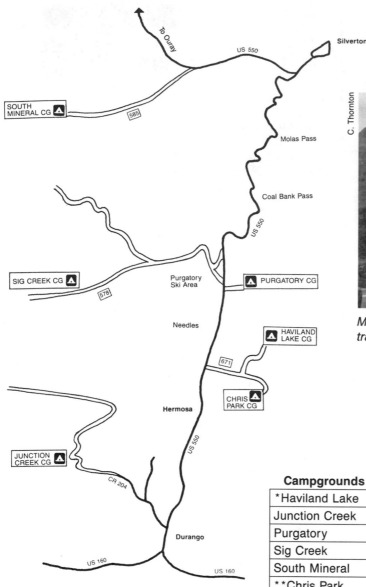

For Information

Animas Ranger District
110 West 11th Street
Durango, CO 81301
(303) 247-4874

Mountain passes in Colorado are well marked to keep the traveler informed of elevations and names.

Campgrounds	Elevation (feet)	Camp Units	Drinking Water	Toilets (F = flush; V = vault)	Small Trailers	Fee Area (in season)
*Haviland Lake	8,000	45	X	V	X	X
Junction Creek	7,500	36	X	V	X	X
Purgatory	9,900	14	X	F	X	X
Sig Creek	10,300	9	X	V		
South Mineral	10,300	23	X	F		X
**Chris Park	8,000	3	X	V		X

* On MISTIX reservation system.
** Organizational group camping; by reservation only.

Campground Locations

Junction Creek is northwest of Durango on Junction Creek Road; go 1 mile north of US 550, then 3½ mile northwest on County Road 204 (turn west at 25th St.), then ½ mile northwest on Forest Road

Haviland Lake is 20 miles north of Durango off of US 550; then 1 mile east on Forest Road 671.

Chris Park Organizational Campground is just 1 mile south on Forest Road 166, with access from the Haviland Lake cut-off.

Purgatory is on US 550, 28 miles north of Durango or 22 miles south of Silverton.

Sig Creek is on Forest Road 578 (Hermosa Park Road), 6 miles west of US 550 between Durango and Silverton; the cut-off is 21 miles from Silverton, 29 miles from Durango.

South Mineral is 2 miles northwest of Silverton on US 550, then 5 miles southwest on Forest Road 585.

Dolores Ranger District

Campground Locations

McPhee Reservoir—located north of Dolores off of SH 184. McPhee Recreation Area (also called Mesa Park) is on the south side of the reservoir, 8 miles from Dolores. *House Creek Recreation Area* is on the east side of the reservoir, 12 miles from Dolores; turn off SH 145 at 11th Street in Dolores and travel 6 miles north on Forest Road 526 to House Creek Road (Forest Road 528), turn left and head west to the Recreation Area.

Forks—14 miles northwest of Dolores at the junction of SH 145 and the West Fork Road (Forest Road 535).

Three other campgrounds are located along the West Fork of the Dolores River along Forest Road 535:
  —*Mavreeso* is 6 miles from the road fork.
  —*West Dolores* is 1 mile beyond Mavreeso.
  —*Burro Bridge* is an additional 16 miles, making it 37 miles from Dolores.

Cayton—6 miles north of Rico on SH 145; then turn right on Forest Road 578 and cross the Dolores River to the campground.

The McPhee Reservoir impounds water from the Dolores River. Boating, water skiing, and fishing are enjoyed while looking at the majestic peaks of the San Juan Mountains.

For Information

Dolores Ranger District
100 North 6th
P.O. Box 210
Dolores, CO 81323
(303) 882-7296

Campgrounds	Elevation (feet)	Camp Units	Drinking Water	Toilets (F = flush; V = vault)	Small Trailers	Fee Area (in season)
Burro Bridge	9,000	15	X	V	X	X
*Cayton	9,380	27	X	V	X	X
Forks	7,386	6	X	V	X	X
*House Creek R.A.	6,910	46	X	V	X	X
*Mavreeso	7,600	14	X	V	X	X
*McPhee R.A.	7,100	80	X	F	X	X
West Dolores	7,600	13	X	V	X	X

* On MISTIX reservation system.
  House Creek & Mesa Park also have group campgrounds; reservation required.

REGION 3

Mancos Ranger District

For Information

Mancos Ranger District
41595 East Highway 160
Box 330
Mancos, CO 81328
(303) 533-7716

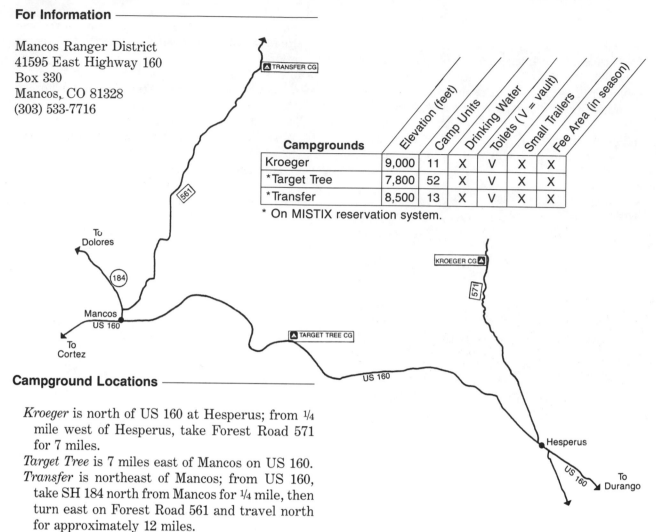

Campgrounds	Elevation (feet)	Camp Units	Drinking Water	Toilets (V = vault)	Small Trailers	Fee Area (in season)
Kroeger	9,000	11	X	V	X	X
*Target Tree	7,800	52	X	V	X	X
*Transfer	8,500	13	X	V	X	X

* On MISTIX reservation system.

Campground Locations

Kroeger is north of US 160 at Hesperus; from ¼ mile west of Hesperus, take Forest Road 571 for 7 miles.

Target Tree is 7 miles east of Mancos on US 160.

Transfer is northeast of Mancos; from US 160, take SH 184 north from Mancos for ¼ mile, then turn east on Forest Road 561 and travel north for approximately 12 miles.

Pagosa Ranger District

For Information

Pagosa Ranger District
P.O. Box 310
Pagosa Springs, CO 81147
(303) 264-2268

Campgrounds	Elevation (feet)	Camp Units	Drinking Water	Toilets (V = vault)	Small Trailers	Fee Area (in season)
Blanco River	7,200	8	X	V	X	
Bridge	7,800	19	X	V	X	X
Cimarrona	8,400	21	X	V	X	X
*East Fork	7,600	26	X	V	X	X
Teal	8,300	15	X	V	X	X
West Fork	8,000	28	X	V	X	X
*Williams Creek	8,200	69	X	V	X	X
Wolf Creek	8,000	26	X	V		X

* On MISTIX reservation system.

Pagosa Ranger District *(continued)*

Campground Locations

Blanco River—10 miles south of Pagosa Springs on US 84; then 3 miles east on Forest Road 656 (Blanco River Road).

Four campgrounds are located on Piedra Road 631, which goes north off of US 160, 2 miles west of Pagosa Springs:

—*Bridge Campground* is 18 miles, and off the road to the east ¼ mile.

—*Williams Creek* is 22 miles, then ½ mile north on Forest Road 640.

—*Teal* is 1½ miles north on Forest Road 640 on Williams Creek Reservoir.

—*Cimarrona* is 4 miles north on Forest Road 640, north of the reservoir.

Three campgrounds are located off of US 160 from Pagosa Springs heading northeast to Wolf Creek Pass:

—*East Fork* is 10 miles from Pagosa Springs; then 1 mile east on Forest Road 667.

—*Wolf Creek* is 12 miles on US 160; then 1 mile north on Forest Road 648 (West Fork Road).

—*West Fork* is beyond Wolf Creek Campground; go 2 miles northwest on Forest Road 648 from US 160.

. . . a typical Colorado river.

Have you noticed how many folks camp in pairs?

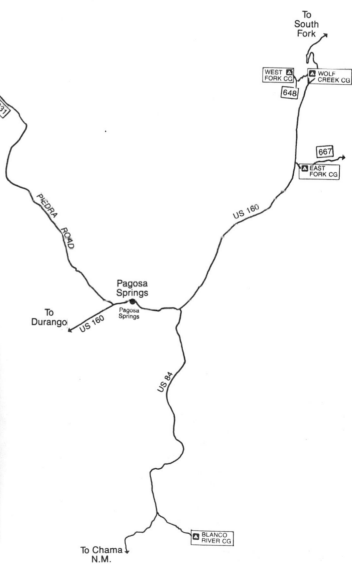

REGION 3

Pine Ranger District

For Information

Pine Ranger District
367 South Pearl Street
P.O. Box 439
Bayfield, CO 81122
(303) 884-2512

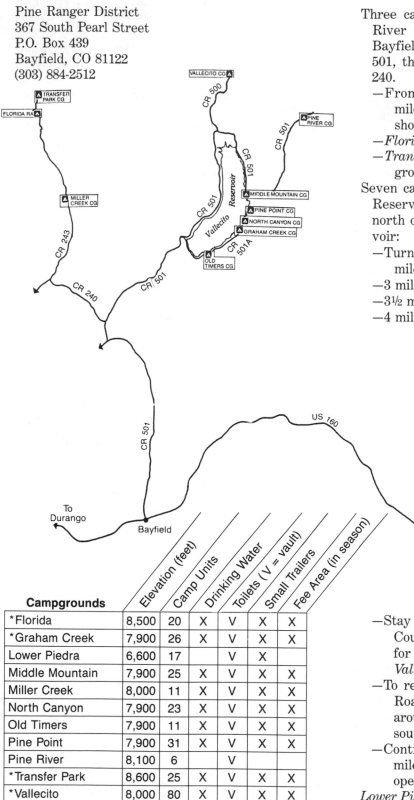

Campground Locations:

Three campgrounds are located in the Florida River drainage near Lemon Reservoir; from Bayfield, travel 11 miles north on County Road 501, then 3 miles northwest on County Road 240.

—From that intersection, *Miller Creek* is 2 miles north on County Road 243 (on east shore of Lemon Reservoir).

—*Florida* is 2 miles beyond.

—*Transfer Park* is 1 mile beyond Florida Campground.

Seven campgrounds are located in the Vallecito Reservoir area; from Bayfield travel 14 miles north on County Road 501 to reach the reservoir:

—Turn right on County Road 501A and go 2 miles to reach *Old Timers;*

—3 miles to reach *Graham Creek.*

—3½ miles to reach *North Canyon.*

—4 miles to reach *Pine Point.*

Campgrounds	Elevation (feet)	Camp Units	Drinking Water	Toilets (V = vault)	Small Trailers	Fee Area (in season)
*Florida	8,500	20	X	V	X	X
*Graham Creek	7,900	26	X	V	X	X
Lower Piedra	6,600	17		V	X	
Middle Mountain	7,900	25	X	V	X	X
Miller Creek	8,000	11	X	V	X	X
North Canyon	7,900	23	X	V	X	X
Old Timers	7,900	11	X	V	X	X
Pine Point	7,900	31	X	V	X	X
Pine River	8,100	6		V		
*Transfer Park	8,600	25	X	V	X	X
*Vallecito	8,000	80	X	V	X	X

* On MISTIX reservation system.

—Stay on the west side of the reservoir on County Road 501 for 4½ miles; then north for 2½ miles on County Road 500 to reach *Vallecito Campground.*

—To reach *Middle Mountain,* stay on County Road 501 for 3 more miles as the road heads around the top of the lake, east and then south.

—Continue on County Road 501 for 4 more miles to reach *Pine River,* a small undeveloped campground.

Lower Piedra is 1 mile north of the town of Chimney Rock on Forest Road 621.

Uncompahgre National Forest

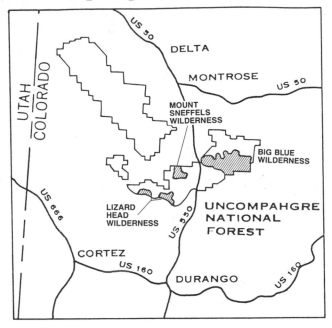

For Information

Grand Mesa-Uncompahgre and Gunnison
  National Forests Headquarters
2250 Highway 50
Delta, CO 81416
(303) 874-7691

Wilderness Areas

Big Blue Wilderness encompasses more than
98,000 acres on the Uncompahgre National Forest. Elevations within the wilderness range
from 8,400 to over 14,000 feet. Over 75 miles of
constructed trails are available for both foot
and horse travel. Normally, the Big Blue area is
snow free from mid-July to September. Some
points of interest in the Big Blue are Uncompahgre Peak (14,309 feet), Wetterhorn Peak
(14,015 feet), Matterhorn Peak, Coxcomb Peak,
Silver Peak, Slide Lake, Big Blue Creek and
The Bridge of Heaven.

Lizard Head Wilderness, north of Rico, encompasses 40,000 acres. This wilderness area is
popular with climbers. Within the area, the San
Miguel Mountains consist of two distinct clusters of peaks. The eastern cluster, informally
called the Wilson Group, contains Mount Wilson
(14,246 feet), El Diente Peak (14,159 feet),
Wilson Peak (14,017 feet), and South Wilson
(14,110 feet). Two miles east is the spectacular
landmark of Lizard Head, a nearly vertical rock
spire that rises 300 feet from a conical base to

13,113 feet. A saddle two miles in length separates the eastern cluster from the western cluster of peaks called the Dolores Peak Group, a
smaller cluster of three peaks which reach a
maximum elevation of 13,290 feet at Dolores
Peak.

Mt. Sneffels Wilderness encompasses more than
16,500 acres on the Uncompahgre National Forest. Elevations within the wilderness range
from 9,600 feet to 14,150 feet. There are over 10
miles of constructed trails. Normally, the
Mount Sneffels area is snow free from mid-July
to September; however some stream crossings
on the Blue Lakes trail may be difficult to cross
in early summer due to high water levels. Some
points of interest in Mount Sneffels are Blue
Lakes and Mount Sneffels (14,150 feet).

*Sunshine Campground offers spectacular views of Lizard
Head Pass and several of the "fourteeners" in the area.*

Location

Uncompahgre National Forest is located in the
southwestern portion of the state; US 550, between
Durango and Montrose passes through a portion;
historic Ouray and Telluride are both within the forest. The mountains are magnificent, with high, rugged alpine peaks and the Uncompahgre Plateau, a
vast uplift, offers unparalleled views in all directions. The Gunnison, Grand Mesa and Uncompahgre national forests were administratively combined in 1976.

REGION 3

Grand Junction Ranger District

For Information

Grand Junction Ranger District
764 Horizon Drive, Room 115
Grand Junction, CO 81506
(303) 242-8211

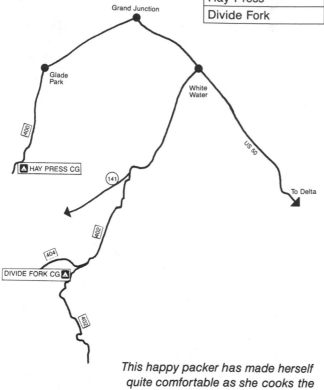

Campgrounds	Elevation (feet)	Camp Units	Drinking Water	Toilets (V = vault)	Small Trailers
Hay Press	9,300	11		V	X
Divide Fork	9,200	11	X	V	X

This happy packer has made herself quite comfortable as she cooks the evening meal in the high country.

Campground Locations

Hay Press—10 miles southwest of Grand Junction via SH 340, through Glade Park (due south of Colorado National Monument); then 20 miles south on Forest Road 400; campground is near Fruita Reservoir.

Divide Fork—from Whitewater on US 50 southeast of Grand Junction, turn southwest on SH 141 and travel 13 miles; then 15 miles southwest on Forest Road 402.

N. L. Gilchrest

Norwood Ranger District

For Information

Norwood Ranger District
1760 East Grand Avenue
P.O. Box 388
Norwood, CO 81423
(303) 327-4261

Campgrounds	Elevation (feet)	Camp Units	Drinking Water	Toilets (V = vault)	Small Trailers	Fee Area (in season)
*Matterhorn	9,480	23	X	V	X	X
Sunshine	9,560	15	X	V	X	X

* On MISTIX reservation system.

Campground Locations

Matterhorn—10 miles southwest of Telluride on SH 145.

Sunshine—8 miles southwest of Telluride on SH 145.

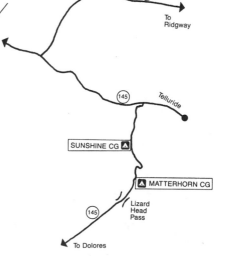